Insulting ENGLISH

ALSO BY PETER NOVOBATZKY AND AMMON SHEA

●●●

Depraved English

ST. MARTIN'S PRESS

NEW YORK

Insulting ENGLISH

●●●

PETER NOVOBATZKY

and

AMMON SHEA

www.stmartins.com

Illustrations courtesy of the New York Public
Library Picture Collection

Production Editor: David Stanford Burr

Library of Congress Cataloging-in-Publication Data

Novobatzky, Peter.
    Insulting English / Peter Novobatzky and
Ammon Shea.—1st ed.
        p.   cm.
    Includes bibliographical references.
    ISBN 0-312-27208-1
    1. English language—Slang—Dictionaries.
2. English language—Obscene words—
Dictionaries.   3. Invective—Dictionaries.
I. Shea, Ammon.   II. Title.

    PE3721 .N68 2001
    427—dc21   2001019150

First Edition: June 2001

10   9   8   7   6   5   4   3   2   1

INTRODUCTION

At no time in history has a word book devoted exclusively to insults been more sorely needed than today. More than ever before, the world abounds with offensive, annoying, and pathetic people. You have to put up with them—why not know the correct words with which to describe them?

As a speaker of English, you're in luck. No other language is as large, as descriptive, or as splenetic. There seems to be an English word for nearly every type of insult-worthy person under the sun. A multitude of terms for idiots of every stripe; a legion of words to poke fun at the ugly, the pompous, the overweight, and the ill-endowed. From *conky* (a big-nosed person) to *quibberdick* (a nasty quibbler), from *naffin* (a near-idiot) to *nullimitus* (a male virgin), from *raddled* (aged and worsened from debauchery) to *ripesuck* (one who is easily bribed), every possible target of invective has its place.

Our first book, *Depraved English*, focused on the perverse, unseemly, and disgusting side of the language. By contrast, *Insulting English* seeks to deliver the perfect epithet for every occasion. Its pages are alive with maniacs, cowards, boors, slobs, outcasts, villains, fanatics, blowhards, misers, fusspots, saps, compulsives, hacks, and spongers. Some of these people are unpleasant; others are merely unfortunate. All of them are excellent targets of ridicule. Male and female, young and old, fat and skinny—we do not discriminate. The greedy, the corrupt, the unlucky, the mean, the loud, the smelly, the lazy, the vain, the pushy, the violent, the servile, the sex-crazed, the ambitious, the argumentative, and the sensitive are all included here.

Many of the words in *Insulting English* are best when employed in a literal sense, while others are most insulting when used metaphorically, or as exaggerations. Of course, the average reader cannot be expected to memorize every word in the book, or to carry it around with him or her everywhere (although it *will* fit in a coat pocket). Still, we hope that at least a few of the entries will resonate enough to be remembered later. That way, when your cashier turns out to be an acalculiac.[1] or there is a cachinnator[2] at your birthday party—even if your date is a diamerdis[3]—you will not splutter in vain for want of the proper word.

While *Insulting English* will be a useful resource for verbal aggressors, it is mainly concerned with describing the world and the people in it with the most precise terminology. In the end, the most devastating insult is nothing more than an accurate—if unflattering—description of a person's faults, defects, or shortcomings. Accordingly, most of the words in this book have very specific definitions, such as "a woman who talks too much" (*chaterestre*), "a man who wears too much cologne" (*muscod*), or "a person who shouts all the

---

[1] One who cannot count or do simple math.
[2] One who laughs loudly or excessively.
[3] A man who is covered in feces.

time" (*klazomaniac*). Such people exist, do they not? To have words for them is only natural. Fairly may we call these words insults, but they are also just descriptions of reality.

You may have had the experience of learning a new word, only to immediately encounter it in many unexpected places. While even the best-known words contained herein (*myrmidon*,[4] for example) are obscure enough that you will rarely see them in print, in *life* your eyes will be opened to startling new insights after reading this book. For once a word like *shotclog*[5] becomes lodged in your brain, you will begin to notice that which it describes popping up everywhere. And just imagine: Thanks to the book you now hold, you will be able to share your unpleasant and cutting new observations with all your friends and enemies. Such are the joys of *Insulting English*.

---

[4] A fanatically obedient follower.
[5] An unpleasant drinking companion, tolerated only because he is buying the drinks.

A NOTE ON THE ENTRIES

We are not professional etymologists or lexicographers. We simply enjoy combing through dictionaries, lexicons, and other word books, looking for obscure and interesting words. Every entry in *Insulting English* is a real English word. There are no slang words, and no neologisms—only actual, legitimate English words. Our sources are listed in the bibliography at the back of the book. The pronunciation guides (and they are only crude guides) are intended for American accents. The sentences demonstrating the words in action relate fictional situations and appear here for the first time.

Insulting
ENGLISH

· A ·

ablutophobic /ab LOOT o FO bik/ adj ● Pathologically afraid of bathing.

[Latin *ablutio* a washing + Greek *phobos* fear]

"To punish him for committing the unnatural act with the chalkboard eraser, Mrs. Schneider forced Henry to sit every day next to the **ablutophobic** girl, the one with the thick pigtails and the faint but unmistakable odor of old sausage about her."

compare **odorivector, stinkard**

abydocomist /ab ee do CO mist/ n ● A liar who boasts of his or her falsehood.

"There were lots of **abydocomists** working the phones at the underground telemarketing firm, but none could top Neville, who would cheerfully swindle a widowed grand-mother out of her annuity fund and then climb atop his desk and trumpet, 'I am the king of the lying worms!' "

compare **fissilingual**

acalculiac /ay kal KOOL ee ak/ n ● Someone who cannot count or do simple math.

"Mortimer could remember exactly when he became disgusted with being a high school math teacher. It was the day he met with the principal to discuss the **acalculiacs** in his freshman class, and the bureaucrat kept whispering: *'Lower the bar, Mort! Lower the bar!'* "

compare agrammaticist

acrotophiliac /uh CRO toe FEEL ee ak/ n ● A person who is sexually attracted to the stumps of amputees.

One of the first words in the book, and already the authors are making fun of the infirm. It doesn't seem quite fair; after all, an amputee needs love as much as the next person. To help make it up to our lesser-limbed friends, we have decided to throw them a bone, in the form of a list detailing the correct word for every different type of person strangely and powerfully aroused by the absence of an appendage.

acrotomophiliac—One who enjoys fantasizing that his or her sexual partner is an amputee.

ameliotist—A person who is sexually attracted to an amputee as a whole, not just to his or her stump.

apotemnophiliac—One who fantasizes about being an amputee; one who schemes to amputate some part of his or her body in order to gain sexual pleasure.

monopediomaniac—Someone with a sexual attraction or psychological dependence on a one-legged person.

compare dysmorphophiliac

adulterine /ad ULT er een/ n ● A person born of an adulterous union.

The distinction between an **adulterine** and a *bastard* is that a bastard is simply the offspring of unwed parents, while an **adulterine** is the issue of an **adulterous** union; that is, one involving folks who are married, just not to each other. Both terms derived much of their original sting from conventional attitudes, grounded in religion, toward marriage and sin. *Bastard*, however, has triumphed by evolving into a broader definition. Nowadays, calling someone a *bastard* does not necessarily mean that the person was born out of wedlock, just that he or she is mean and despicable. But while *bastard* is now a commonly used insult, **adulterine** remains stuck in its original, specific meaning, and is not often used.

compare **gandermooner, uzzard, wetewold**

aerocolpos /air o KOLE pose/ n ● Vaginal flatulence; air or gas trapped in the vagina.

[Greek *aer* air + *kolpos* bosom or fold]

Yes, there exists a technical term for this unmentionable occurrence. So why doesn't anyone know what to properly call it? Other unappealing bodily functions are known by their official names; why does **aerocolpos** have to go by *quiff* (meaning, literally, "puff of air")? Could it be that this concept still elicits some feelings of queasiness or embarrassment with certain people? Remember, gentle reader: **aerocolpos** is as natural as breathing. Just because it often occurs during sex doesn't mean it is something to be ashamed of. (However, this does not mean that the authors cannot poke fun at it. . . .)

compare eproctolagniac

ageustia /*ay GOOSE tee uh*/ n • Absence of a sense of taste; complete or partial loss of the sense of taste.

[*a* (neg.) + Greek *geusis* taste]

A metaphorical gem, and a useful code word to share with a friend. Symptoms of this actual medical condition include a tolerance for dubious foods, and the wearing of stripes with plaid.

"Either Janice's new in-laws possessed a highly evolved sense of humor, or they suffered from severe **ageustia.** How else to explain their wedding present, a neon cuckoo clock that blurted the theme songs from seventies sitcoms every quarter hour?"

compare bedizen

agramaticist /*ay gram AT iss ist*/ n • One suffering from *agrammaticism*: the inability to form sentences.

"Nathan was a lifelong **aggramaticist,** but was able to put this shortcoming to good use in his chosen career: politics. Speaking entirely in disconnected sound bites, he truly was the candidate for the twenty-first century."

compare acalculiac

agitatrix /*aj ih TAY trix*/ n • A female agitator; a woman who agitates.

Men can recognize the dreaded **agitatrix** by these telltale utterances: "Does this dress make me look fat?" "Do you think she's cute?" "Why don't you tell me you love me?" and the ever-popular "You're not allowed to fart in bed."

compare baratress

aidle /AY dll/ v • "To earn one's bread indifferently well." (Charles Mackay's *Lost Beauties of the English Language*, 1874)

"**Aidling** away the months selling greeting cards door-to-door, Michelle didn't care if she sold two, twelve, or none at all. She did enjoy taking three-hour lunches, however, and could often be seen sitting in a quiet and shady corner of the park catching up on her reading."

compare eyeservant, ploiter

alacuoth /al uh KOO oth/ n • Involuntary defecation during sex.

Befouling oneself is difficult to cope with in the best of circumstances—how much more so with such unfortunate timing.

No doubt many readers will immediately cast **alacuoth** onto that dung heap of the mind where one chucks all the unpleasant things one would rather forget. But while it may be one of those words of which it is happiest to remain ignorant, it demands inclusion in any unflinching discussion of the descriptive capacities of the English language.

"Milo knew what he was looking for in a woman, and when he finally found one who didn't seem to mind his chronic **alacuoth**, he slapped a ring on her finger in two whisks of a lamb's tail."

compare dyspareunia, sterky

allorgasmia */al or GAZ mee uh/* n • Fantasizing about someone other than one's partner during sex.

Allorgasmia is not usually something one openly discusses with one's sexual partner. But it is fairly common. What's more, the spice it brings to the bedroom probably saves more relationships than all the marital therapists west of the Missippippi. So, the next time **allorgasmia** causes the supermarket checkout girl or delivery boy to make a guest appearance in your bed—er, *head*—try not to feel too guilty about it.

compare anagapesis

alothen */AL o then/* v • To grow disgusting.

From people to cultural phenomena to leftover tuna casserole, there are so many potential uses for the word **alothen** that the reader is encouraged to let his or her imagination run wild.

compare turdefy

ambisinister */am bi SIN ist er/* adj • Lacking manual dexterity with both hands; having "two left hands."

[Latin *ambi* both + *sinister* left]

"Spencer, the airport baggage-handler, had the perfect job for someone as **ambisinister** as himself. He solved the problem of punching the clock by holding his time card in his teeth, but the mandatory coffee break still posed special hazards for him, and he kept a rubberized poncho in his locker for the occasion."

compare looby

amourette /*am oor ET*/ n • A petty or insignificant love affair.

"Edward Kleeger, titan of business and industry, was devastated when the dominatrix he wined and dined on weekends told him that she was moving on, saying: 'You were never more than an **amourette,** Ed, and not a very enjoyable one, at that.' "

amplexus /*am PLEX us*/ n • The mating embrace of a toad or a frog.

From the endlessly descriptive world of biology comes this sparkler of a word. Since it is common enough to refer to a repulsive person as a toad, a figurative use for **amplexus** logically presents itself.

"The last thing I remembered from that evening was hiding in the men's room to escape the attentions of the vile Mrs. Flamm. Early the next morning I awoke in a strange bed with a terrible hangover, only to realize with horror that I was firmly caught in her **amplexus.**"

compare **strene**

anaclitic /*an uh KLIT ik*/ adj • 1) Overly dependent on others for emotional support. 2) Overly dependent on one's mother.

[Greek *ana* again, up, back + *klinein* to lean]

"Everyone warned Ellen that she was coddling her teenage son, but she just couldn't resist when he whined from bed for a sponge bath, and so his **anaclitic** dependency continued to deepen."

As she dries off her husband's tears,
Beth wrinkles her nose up and sneers,
"Not to be a critic,
*but you're still **anaclitic,***
and your mother's been dead now for years."
compare **rectopathic**

anagapesis */an uh gap EE sis/* n ● A loss of feelings for one formerly loved.

This is a terrible yet useful word. For all those who at one time or another have clumsily and ineffectually struggled to say, "I don't love you anymore," without having to actually *say* it, don't be fooled: "I *love* you, I'm just not *in* love with you" is a horrible thing to tell somebody. To avoid this and other clichés, it is better to tell one's ex-to-be that one has been stricken with **anagapesis**—then get the hell out of there before he or she reaches for the dictionary.

compare **allorgasmia, anaxiphilia**

anaxiphilia */lan AX if EEL ee uh/* n ● The act of falling in love with the wrong person.

Another in a long list of depressingly common human afflictions, **anaxiphilia** can befall anyone. While this word is not an insult per se, it can be used to gently rib—or brutally make fun of—someone who has recently had his or her heart crushed.

compare **anagapesis**

androgalactozemia */AN dro gal AK toe ZEE mee uh/* n ● Secretion of milk from the male breast.

[Greek *andros* man + *gala* milk + *zemia* loss]

Could any creature be more deserving of ridicule than the man with **androgalactozemia?** Probably not. The only consolation for the poor slob with this condition is that since most people don't believe such a thing can actually happen, when confronted with it they will probably be too perplexed to laugh, at least at first.

"Raymond eschewed doctors, and working with a homemade surgical kit of knitting needles, rubber plugs, and Super Glue, bravely dealt with his **androgalactozemia** on his own."
compare **pogogniasis**

anhedonia */an hed O nee uh/* n • The inability to experience feelings of pleasure or happiness.

[*an* (neg.) + Greek *hedone* pleasure + *ia*]

As people with **anhedonia** are quite likely to make life miserable for everyone around them, this is a word worth knowing.

"Audrey surrendered to her **anhedonia** and married a shriveled and whining orthodontist. Why not? It was impossible for her to be happy anyway. At least this way she got full dental coverage."
compare **antithalian**

animalist */AN im al ist/* n • A person who engages in bestiality.

"As a boxer, Hector 'The **Animalist**' Suarez was rather proud of his moniker, thinking that it doubtless made reference to some boundless crop of energy that he possessed. In reality, it stemmed more from his nightly habit of drinking

ANIMALIST

himself insensate enough to couple with anything with a pulse."

compare **anthropozoophilic, avisodomy**

ankyloproctia /*an kil o PROK tee uh*/ n ● A severe constriction of the anus.

[Greek *ankylos* bent, crooked + *proktos* anus]

The perfect word to describe a tight-ass.

"Donald's **ankyloproctia** came as a terrible blow to the pudgy gourmand. His doctors had now restricted him to a diet consisting entirely of foods that could easily pass through his narrowed system, such as baby food and overripe bananas."

compare **sterky**

anorgasmic */AN or GAZ mik/* adj • Failing to achieve orgasm during sex.

"While the **anorgasmic** relations he suffered with his fifth wife were not something Simon would have wished upon himself, they were certainly an improvement over the situation with his previous brides, all of whom had refused to sleep with him at all."

compare **dyspareunia**

anteric */lanTER ik/* adj • Seeking vengeance for slighted love.

"In an **anteric** rage, Sarah decided that slashing the tires of her ex-boyfriend's pickup truck just wasn't enough. So she set it ablaze and flung herself on top of it."

compare **anaxiphilia**

anthropozoophilic */AN thro PO zoo FILL ik/* adj • Attracted to both people and animals.

[Greek *anthropos* man + *zoon* animal + *philein* to love]

While this term is primarily employed to describe insects, we are confident that some of our more deviant readers will find another use for it.

" 'Any port in a storm,' thought the **anthropozoophilic** Edmund, after the third and last farmer's daughter rebuffed his licentious advances, and he was told in no uncertain terms to go and sleep in the barn."

compare **animalist, avisodomy, omnifutuant**

antinomian */an tee NOME ee an/* n • A person who believes that faith in Christ frees him or her from moral and legal obligations.

"No one in his small Southern town objected to Lloyd not paying taxes, using a homemade license plate, or flying his own separatist flag proclaiming his trailer home/arsenal to be a 'principality of Jesus.' But there had to be a limit to religious expression, and when the zealous **antinomian** cut the ticket line at the high school football game, a lynching party quickly coalesced out of the throng."

compare eisegetical, tartuffe

antithalian /*an tee THALE ee an*/ adj ● Disapproving of laughter or festivity.

"Many citizens were distressed by the law-and-order mayor's **antithalian** crusade of ticketing anyone who laughed in public ('It's a quality-of-life issue,' he insisted). But no one could deny that the policy, when enforced, lent the city something of a genteel and cultivated air."

compare anhedonia, cachinnator

antivitruvian /*an ti vit ROO vee an*/ adj ● Taking pleasure in destroying architectural monuments.

This wonderfully specific word comes to us from the name of a famed Roman architect, Vitruvius. While it is unlikely that the reader will ever have an opportunity to rise at a town meeting and, raising his or her voice in a stentorian fashion, cry: "You, sir, are nothing more than a base and vile **antivitruvianist!**," it is still a word that every lover of fine buildings should know. Certainly there seem to be an inordinate number of these despicable creatures in circulation today.

"Once he promised them a fifty-dollar tax credit, most of

the townsfolk came around to supporting the councilman's **antivitruvian** plan to rip down the seventeenth-century town hall and replace it with a new cinderblock courthouse."

compare **grimthorpe**

apoglutic /*ap o GLOO tik*/ adj ● Having a tiny rump.

For those readers who prefer rear ends that are built for comfort and not for speed, the authors offer **apoglutic** for use as an insult.

"As a personal trainer to the stars, Rolanda was renowned for her ability to render anyone **apoglutic**. Indeed, she refused to consider a client a success until her posterior was skinny enough to make sitting on it decidedly uncomfortable."

compare **kakopygian, unipygic**

apophallation /*ap o fal AY shun*/ n ● Among slugs, the practice of chewing off a partner's penis following sex.

Slugs are endowed with what is proportionally one of the largest penises in the animal kingdom; an eight-inch slug can have a member that is just as long as he is. There is a terrible downside to such phallic magnificence, however. Every so often a slug will get stuck. Imagine: you're hot and sweaty, the deed has been done, and you really want nothing so much as a cigarette and a shower, but your partner just can't withdraw. Can you really blame the slug for chewing it off?

"Mr. Duval was a dedicated, if slightly unstable, health teacher. Nevertheless, there was some degree of controversy among the local parents when he began showing nature films of animals engaging in **apophallation** to his sophomore class as a deterrent to sexual activity."

compare dyspareunia

assot /*ASS ot*/ v ● To make a fool of.

"Her first day at her first job out of college, and Kirsten had thoroughly **assotted** herself. They'd told her to 'dress her best' for work, and so she had donned the only finery she had: her bright green prom dress from five years ago. Oh, the humiliation when they sent her home in tears!"

atolmia /*ay TOLE mee uh*/ n ● Impotence in a man due to lack of confidence.

"Operating according to the credo 'You've got to break a man all the way down before you can build him up again,' the Longwell Institute for Male Pleasure (L.I.M.P.) racked up several successes—as well as a large number of spectacular failures—with its 'tough love' approach to curing **atolmia."**

compare anorgasmic, peniculas

autosmia /*aw TOZ mee uh*/ n ● The smelling of one's own bodily odors.

[Greek *auto* self + *osme* smell]

"Jared was an outcast his whole life, somehow never grasping that his erotic obsession with **autosmia** was part of the reason why."

compare odorivector

autotheist /*aw toe THEE ist*/ n ● One who believes that he or she is God.

"Fisk's many minions were accustomed to the billionaire **autotheist's** monstrous egotism. It was his complete neglect of even the most basic personal hygiene that took a bit more getting used to."

compare **pleionosis**

avisodomy /*uh VIZ o dome ee*/ n ● The act of having sex with a bird.

Live long enough and there will come a time when you desperately wish that you knew a word that means to have sex with a bird. Bereft of such knowledge, most people will sputter and cast about in vain before coming up with a colorful but crude expression, such as 'duck-fucker.'

Avisodomy covers sexual congress with any type of bird, but it is most commonly applied to fowl.

"Although they were the only house on campus that insisted their pledges be videotaped engaging in **avisodomy,** Sigma Tau Delta had such a degree of social cachet, and threw such splendid mixers, that they had more pledges clamoring to join than any other three fraternities combined."

compare **animalist, anthropozoophilic**

• B •

badling /*BAD ling*/ n • A man who is effeminate or worthless.

[Old English *baedling* a womanish man]

"After the storm, all the women and children bailed desperately to keep the lifeboat from sinking. Not Lucas the **badling,** though. He just hopped up and down in the stern, flapping his arms in the air and exclaiming, 'Oh my, oh, my!' "

compare **subvirate**

barathrum /*BA rath rum*/ n • 1. An insatiable glutton. 2. An extortionist who will not be satisfied.

So called after the **Barathrum**, a pit outside the city of Athens into which criminals, alive and dead, were thrown.

compare **gulchin, rabiator**

baratress /*BA ruh tress*/ n • A female quarreler.

She may just as easily pick on a woman, but like her cousin

BARATHRUM

the **agitatrix,** the **baratress** strikes a special fear into the heart of many a man. For who knows what comment, innocuous though it might seem, will raise the hackles and invoke the ire of a **baratress?** It could be something innocent, such as "That dress looks good on you," or it could be an incredibly stupid statement, like "I had lunch with my ex-girlfriend today."

compare **agitatrix, breedbate, quibberdick**

barkled /*BARK ld*/ adj • Encrusted with dirt; used especially to describe a person's skin.

"Rich though she was, Hetty still fancied that society owed her something, and she tried to bilk the state out of as much welfare as she could. There was always a mad rush to get her children looking as **barkled** and ill clad as possible each time the caseworker came to her door."

compare trugabelly

barlichood /BAR lich ood/ adj • Drunk and mean.

"All the regulars at McKenna's looked forward to seven o'clock with keen anticipation. For that was when old Mr. Gleason, thoroughly **barlichood** with cheap gin, would begin hollering with rage at the nightly news on the TV over the bar."

compare debacchate, zowerswopped

barrator /BA ruh tor/ n • An ambulance-chasing lawyer.

Yes, there exists a time-honored term for this bottom-feeder.

There is nothing so nice
as a slick patch of ice
on the sidewalk
*to the **barrator**.*
For ultimately, all misery
is useful for lining his pockets more.

With great indignation, and fury unbridled,
he gets you the monies to which you're entitled.

compare bdelloid, leguleian, rabulistic

bathetic /buh THET ik/ adj • Falsely sentimental.

"Samantha was truly sickened by the way her weasel-like boyfriend went to such great lengths to avoid taking the blame for anything, frequently waxing **bathetic** and crying crocodile tears. After one such episode too many, she dumped a pot of boiling spaghetti water on his foot and announced that she was leaving."

compare rectopathic

bdelloid /DELL oid/ adj ● Resembling a leech.

[Greek *bdella* leech + *oid*]

"Paige's **bdelloid** younger brother refused to get a job, arguing that he hadn't 'found the right thing yet.' Instead, he continued to siphon bed and board off of his friends and a roster of fleeting lovers."

compare barrator

beadledom /BEE dul dum/ n ● Petty and stupid officialdom.

Nonsensical rules stubbornly adhered to are one hallmark of **beadledom,** the culture of which is seemingly always expanding. But **beadledom** is not just about red tape. It is a state of mind: the standard mode of thinking for most of the lazy, stupid, mean, and self-important people who staff our bureaucracies.

"The insufferable **beadledom** of the snotty teenage parking-lot attendant made Joyce see red. After reparking her pickup truck five times within the white lines—each time somehow unsatisfactorily—she grimly backed up over his little hut in revenge."

compare spuddle

beau-nasty /bow NASS tee/ n ● A slovenly fop.

The correlation between vanity and personal hygiene is sometimes a tenuous one.

"Armand the **beau-nasty** was almost ready for his blind date. He donned his wrinkled but expensive shirt, slipped on his malodorous Italian shoes, and admired his reflection in the mirror. Noticing a clot of spackling compound in his hair, he donned a fedora at a rakish angle and strutted out the door."

compare **muscod**

bedizen /*bee DIZ en*/ v ● To dress in a flashy or vulgar manner.

[*be-+ dizen* to dress gaudily]

"Most of the time, our aunt Martha was a quietly unattractive person. When fully **bedizened** for a special occasion, however, such as one of her semiannual dates with the local knacker, she transformed into a scarecrowlike monstrosity."

compare **callomaniac, mab**

bedung /*bee DUNG*/ v ● 1) To cover with shit. 2) To daub with shit.

There are many words in English having to do with excremental matter, but it is rare to come across one with such delicate shadings of meaning. Useful for describing everything from the object that has been daubed with the lightest and most gauzy shadings of ordure to the farmer who has had his fertilizer tractor overturn on him, **bedung** is special.

compare **bemute, bepiss, bespawled, bevomit**

begrutten /*bee GROO ten*/ adj ● Having one's face swollen or disfigured from weeping.

[*be-* + *grutten* (past participle of *greet*, meaning to weep)]

"Shortly after the evangelist was indicted for fraud, his fleshy and perpetually **begrutten** wife began appearing regularly on television, exhorting the faithful to pray for a mistrial."

compare **plorabunde, rectopathic**

bemute /*bee MUTE*/ v ● To drop dung on from above, as does a bird.

When compiling a book of odd English words, it never hurts to throw in one or two denoting the act of dropping shit on someone from a considerable height.

"In a move that was arguably more mentally unbalanced than it was cunning, Gallhager had finally found the perfect way to avoid traffic tickets when he ventured into the city. Each night he would park his car directly under the lamppost where all the pigeons sat; after several weeks, no traffic agent in the world would go near his **bemuted** vehicle."

compare **feculent**

bepiss /*bee PISS*/ v ● To urinate upon; to wet with urine.

No surprises as far as the definition of this word is concerned.

"As headmaster of the boarding academy for troublesome children with parents of means, Quimby didn't fall for any of that mamby-pamby, New Age, spare-the-rod business. When little Richie Snead **bepissed** his bed, he stripped the lad down to his undies, painted his face black, and forced him to parade in front of the student body carrying a sign reading, 'I Am a Filthy Little Bastard.' "

compare **pissburnt**

bespawled */bee SPALD/* adj ● Spattered with saliva.

This is another of the infamous *be*-words (**bevomit, bepiss,** etc.) that add so much color to our language.

"As part of the republic's new 'war on corruption,' public officials convicted of accepting bribes were forced to run a gauntlet of angry citizens while naked. While running, they were exposed to the most hideous **bespawling** imaginable."
compare **screable, sialismus**

bevomit */bee VOM it/* v ● To vomit upon.

There are two cardinal rules where **bevomiting** is concerned. 1) It is better to **bevomit** someone other than yourself. 2) Never **bevomit** someone larger than you.

In his *Dictionary of the Vulgar Tongue*, Sir Francis Grose lists a wonderful phrase for the **bevomiter:** Admiral of the Narrow Seas ("one who from drunkenness vomits into the lap of the person sitting opposite to him").
compare **emetomaniac, hyperemian**

bivirist */BIH vir ist/* n ● A woman who enjoys sex with two men at the same time.

"Was the electorate more concerned with her stand on the issues, or were such revelations simply less damaging to a politician with a *conservative* record? Whatever the reason, the candidate's salad days as a confirmed **bivirist** never became a major issue in her campaign."

blatherskite */BLATH er skite/* n ● A boaster; a loudmouth. A blathering fellow.

" 'Simmer down, you **blatherskites!**' yelled the cathouse madam at the posse of rowdy, whiskey-soaked cowboys in her waiting room. 'The next one of y'all starts trouble I swear won't be able to piss for a week without hollerin'!' "

compare **cacafuego, ventose**

blowmaunger /*BLOW mong er*/ n ● A person who is fat to the point that his or her cheeks are puffed out.

"Climbing up the long flight of stairs leading to his podiatrist's office was always a strenuous chore for Chester the **blowmaunger.** Today it was harder than ever for him to catch his breath, what with his cheeks being full of chunks of chocolate éclair. Only the prospect of those root-beer-flavored lollipops at the top gave him the determination to press on."

compare **brephopolysarcia, porknell, pursy**

blowze /*BLOUZE*/ n ● "A fat, red flaccid bloted [sic] wench, or one whose whole head is dressed like a slattern." (Nathaniel Bailey's *Dictionary of the English Tongue*, 1761.)

"For those magical ten minutes, the inexorable march of time rolled back for the boozy old **blowze** in the hotel piano bar, as she warbled along mistily to the strains of her sentimental favorite, 'Send in the Clowns.' "

boodler /*BOOD ler*/ n ● One who happily accepts or offers bribes.

"Busted trying to purchase an illegal substance in Mexico City, Maurice was sure that his political career had come to an end. But in a happy twist of fate, the judge turned out to be an agreeable old **boodler** who was willing to forget about the whole episode in exchange for a small honorarium."

compare **cacique, ripesuck**

brachyphallic /*BRAK ee FAL ik*/ adj ● Having a penis that is very short.

"Swineburne, the **brachyphallic** customs agent, closed his eyes and began to inwardly chant his personal mantra, 'It ain't the size of the boat, it's the motion of the ocean,' as he removed his boxer shorts and entered into his newlywed's embraces for the first time."

compare **macromaniac, micropenis, peniculas, subvirate**

breedbate /*BREED bate*/ n ● One looking for a fight or argument; a troublemaker.

All families have at least one **breedbate**—he or she who insists on talking politics over Thanksgiving dinner, or who gives unwanted advice on whether to circumcise a newborn. What is one to do? For starters, it might pay to become familiar with some of the words in this book. Because if an argument is unavoidable, one might as well get some good digs in.

compare **baratress, quibberdick**

brephopolysarcia /*BREPH o pol ee SAR shuh*/ n ● Excessive fleshiness in an infant.

[Greek *brephos* newborn infant + *poly* many + *sarx* flesh]

All babies are fat. Fat little cheeks, fat little fingers, fat little toes. It helps make them cute, which is the only reason their parents put up with them. (After all, they just cry most of the time, and realistically speaking they won't be good for any kind of heavy labor for at least several years.) For the most part, people seem to love these fat little people, but every once in a while one comes across babies with **brephopolysarcia** that is so striking one has to recoil in horror and wonder: Do even their *parents* think they're cute?

compare **bulchin**

brochity /*BROCH it ee*/ n ● Crookedness of the teeth.

[Latin *brocchitas* a projection of the teeth in animals]

"As the headmistress of the Sterling Thrush Academy for Young Ladies, Wilma Thackleberry prided herself on her ability to transform even the least refined young woman into a paragon of charm. But when she was confronted with Edna, she of the **brochity** grimace (and fat ankles to boot), she simply told the girl to keep her mouth closed at all times and always wear long pants."

compare **gubbertush**

bulchin /*BULCH in*/ n ● A chubby or broad-faced boy.

"Everyone loved Jimmie, the class **bulchin** with a limp. Most of the boys expressed their affection by throwing mud at him, or by taking turns kicking him in the rear end."

compare **brephopolysarcia**

byspel /*BY spel*/ n ● The outcast of a family.

"The **byspel** of his rich and landed clan, young Norton lived alone in a shed, by the woods on the edge of the estate.

He was not invited to meals, and never spoken to. He did not receive an allowance, an education, or familial love of any kind. He prowled about mostly at night, subsisting on roots and the thin gruel put out for the hogs. He wore homespun clothing. And after the big house burned to the ground, taking everyone with it, he inherited every penny of the family fortune."

compare **uzzard**

· C ·

cacafuego /*kak uh FWAY go*/ n ● A braggart; literally, a "shit-fire."

[Spanish *caca* shit + *fuego* fire]

"The drinks kept on coming, and Boris the **cacafuego** continued with his loud, boastful tirades and vulgar gesticulations. No matter; he was about to get his comeuppance—in the form of the beating of his life—from the little old lady quietly sipping her sherry at the end of the bar: the one with the brick in her purse."

compare **blatherskite, ventose**

cachinnator /*KAK in ate or*/ n ● One who laughs loudly, excessively, or for no reason.

[Latin *cachinnare* to laugh aloud]

Unfortunately, this is one of the more necessary words in this lexicon. **Cachinnation** can arise anywhere, at any time, and it is always extremely irritating. Of all the everyday sensory assaults whose source is one's fellow human being, perhaps only a powerful bodily odor is less agreeable than the noise made by the **cachinnator**.

This infernal pest, along with his latest unholy mutation, the **cachinnator** on the cell phone, typically favors enclosed public spaces where many people are gathered together and from which escape is not possible. Who among us has been so lucky as to have not—and recently—cast baleful glances in the vicinity of some shrill and persistent **cachinnator** in our restaurant, theater, bus, or plane?

"Six hours trapped in a car with his **cachinnating,** slightly senile mother-in-law were enough to completely unhinge poor Morton, and he began to tear out his hair in great clumps."

compare **klazomaniac**

cacique /*kuh SEEK*/ n • A corrupt and small-time Latin American political boss.

"United Banana's business motto, 'Find a good **cacique** and stick with him,' was hugely successful and widely imitated in its time."

compare **boodler, ripesuck**

cacozelot /*kak o ZEL ut*/ n • An evil zealot.

" 'One needs to be a bit of a **cacozelot** to succeed in this line of business,' explained Eric's seedy but avuncular supervisor at the fly-by-night investment firm, showing him to his very own cubicle. The young hiree began to feel that he had finally found a home."

cadator /*CAD uh tor*/ n • A beggar who poses as a decayed gentleman.

"Perhaps it was the shambling old beggar's graying temples, which lent him an air of faded dignity, or the tattered suit that had seen better days. Whatever the reason, Angie's heart was touched to the tune of a twenty-dollar bill. Unbeknownst to her, this **cadator's** carefully cultivated aura not only paid for a condo in Miami, but for a growing collection of rare cartoon art as well."

compare **mumblecrust, screeve**

callomaniac /kal o MAY nee ak/ n ● A person under the delusion that he or she is beautiful.

A true sparkler of a word. **Callomaniacs** are common enough, and often painfully easy to spot. They also belong to that peculiar group of people who one doesn't know whether to pity or to despise.

Excepting those few **callomaniacs** with hearts of gold (in whom, beauty being subjective, such self-deception is almost excusable), everyone with this condition should be ridiculed without mercy until disabused of their delusion.

"Ever the **callomaniac,** Gretchen insisted on squeezing her figure, with its grotesque marshmallow-like consistency, into a variety of overly tight pieces of spandex clothing, with the unfortunate result that large pockets of flesh would invariably spill out in bits and pieces."

compare **plutomaniac, sophomaniac**

cantabank /KANT uh bank/ n ● A second-rate singer of ballads.

As everyone who has listened to top-forty radio understands, **cantabank** is still a useful word.

CALLOMANIAC

CANTABANK

"As a manager of **cantabanks,** Murray felt a wave of validation as his latest protégé rose steadily up through the pop charts. All those months scouring mini-mall parking lots for 'that' kid, the one with the piercings and natural sneer that cried out 'Star,' had all been worth it."

compare **windbroach**

catagelophobe /*cat uh GELL o fobe*/ n ● One who is pathologically fearful of being teased.

If you can't make fun of someone with a devastating social illness, who *can* you make fun of?

"Max, the stuttering **catagelophobe,** was hiding in the back of the bus as usual when on board came his worst nightmare: a troop of smart-alecky fourth-graders. Lunging for the emergency brake, he fled the conveyance in a state of high anxiety."

compare **rectopathic**

cepivorous /sep IV or us/ adj ● Feeding on onions.

"Jeanie couldn't stop crying at the funeral, not so much out of grief for the deceased—indeed, she had hardly known him—as because she was seated next to her **cepivorous** uncle Bela."

compare **ranivorous**

chaterestre /CHAT er EST er/ n ● A woman who talks too much; a female chatterer.

That rarest of birds, the woman who talks too much, is a creature shrouded in legend and rarely, if ever, seen. Dim reports from faraway lands will occasionally arise, much akin to those concerning the yeti or the giant killer sloth of South America. Almost inevitably these stories are proven false by even the most casual examination. However, in the extremely unlikely event that the reader should happen upon this chimera, it will perhaps prove useful to be familiar with the correct terminology with which to describe her.

compare **clatterfart**

chichiface /CHI chi face/ n ● A person with a pinched and bony face.

It is always good to have another word at your disposal

with which to describe a pinched and bony face, but the history of this word is more interesting than its definition. It is derived from the French *chichefache* (ugly, thin face). In English literature of the 1300s and 1400s, the *Chichevache* was the name of a fabled monster, perpetually hungry and starved due to the fact that it lived entirely on a diet of patient wives. (Not to be confused with the Bicorne, another fabled monster, which grew fat due to its diet of patient husbands.)

compare **scrag**

chiromaniac /KAI ro MAY nee ak/ n ● A compulsive masturbator.

"The truth was that Jeb Purdy had been injured in a freak yachting accident over the summer holiday. But the vicious gossip at school held that he was a **chiromaniac** whose parents had wrapped his hands in bandages to prevent him from abusing himself in class."

chrematisophiliac /KREM uh tiz o FEEL ee ak/ n ● One who gets aroused from being charged money for sex.

In the vast pantheon of bizarre human sexual predilections, there are more than a few that can be hazardous to one's health. None, however, are as potentially damaging to the *wallet* as **chrematisophilia.**

"How sad that the union of this perfect couple was doomed to fail. They had so much in common—perhaps *too* much, for they were both **chrematisophiliacs,** and trading money back and forth just didn't 'do it' for either of them."

compare **proxenetism**

circumstantiality */SUR cum STANCH ee AL it ee/* n • The inability to separate important from unimportant details when telling a story.

In the medical literature, this psychiatric condition is often associated with symptoms such as confusion, a glazed stare, drooling, and narcolepsy. Not among the sufferers themselves, mind you, but those forced to listen to them.

clarty-paps */CLAR tee paps/* n • A dirty, slovenly wife.

"Being a door-to-door salesman was not as glamorous and carefree as Saunders had pictured it. There had to be something more to life than hawking roach traps to **clarty-papses** with their hair in curlers."

clatterfart */KLAT er fart/* n • A chatterer.

Clatterfart is one of those words that sound a bit worse than they really are. Such words come in handy when one wants to make someone feel bad but can't find anything particularly distasteful about him or her. One should never let such trivial obstacles discourage one from being insulting.

compare **chaterestre**

clinomaniac */KLY no MANE ee ak/* n • One suffering from an excessive desire to stay in bed.

"When the duchess spent a week of her Mediterranean holiday locked up in her hotel room ordering room service, her retinue feared she had become a **clinomaniac.** Only when they caught a glimpse of her virile new paramour through the keyhole did they stop worrying."

COCKALORUM

cockalorum /*kok uh LO rum*/ n • A self-important little man.

"Strutting to and fro in his starched, resplendent little uniform with the plumes on the cap, his pencil mustache quivering as he squeaked redundant orders in a voice even the lowliest private was trained to ignore, the general's **cockalorum** nephew really made quite a spectacle. Unfortunately, as he himself was beginning to realize, he was extremely unlikely to survive the next coup."

compare **beadledom, spuddle**

comprachico /*KOM pruh CHEEK o*/ n • A villain who sells children after first deforming them.

Before casting judgment on the **comprachico,** let the reader look deep within his own soul. For is it not possible that this man is merely trying to make ends meet? Perhaps he wrestled long and hard with his conscience before gravely announcing to his harried wife and three hungry children one night over a nearly empty dinner table: "I've decided to take that job as a **comprachico** Jim offered me down in the village."

compare **dippoldism**

conky /*KONK ee*/ n • A person with a big nose.

Some sources nominate **conky** as a possible root of the pejorative term *honky*, meaning a white person.

"Sir Grossbeak had always been extremely proud of his immense honker; he even had his portrait painted in profile to show it off. When a falconing mishap cost him his prized appendage, he commissioned a magnificent prosthesis to be carved from an elephant's tusk."

coproma /*cop RO muh*/ n • A large clump of compacted feces that can form in the rectum, resembling a tumor.

"Having attended several medical seminars some years in the past, Dorland thought himself up to the task of rectifying his own **coproma** and made an ill-advised attempt at home, with the help of a mirror, some olive oil, and a pair of pinking shears."

compare **scybalous**

crackheaded /*KRAK hed ed*/ adj • Crazy.

Although it certainly looks to be of contemporary coinage, **crackheaded** actually has a pedigree that far precedes the 1980s. There does not seem to be any direct relationship between the terms of then and now. Rather, *crackhead* appears to be a case of a new word arising in the form of an old and venerable one.

compare **mattoid**

creodont /*KREE o dont*/ n • A primitive small-brained animal.

Handsome suitors she had by the score,
and diamond baubles were aught that she wore.
So who could have guessed
that a woman so blessed
*would marry a **creodont** bore?*

crepehanger /*KRAPE hang er*/ n • A pessimistic killjoy.

"It will probably rain," "That's not good for you," or "I saw those shoes on sale for half of what you paid." The

crepehanger always has something deflating to say. This is a pleasingly visual word for a gloomy personality.

compare **marplot, snoutband**

cretinize /KREE tin ize/ v ● To cause to turn into a misshapen idiot dwarf.

It may be best to use this word metaphorically.

"Perhaps it was the gods' way of punishing her for her bad taste in having a Cinderella-themed wedding. *Something* was **cretinizing** the swashbuckling romantic Gloria had married. Now, in what were supposed to be the golden years of their marriage, he would do nothing but sit on the couch all day long, curled over a cheap beer and guffawing at reruns of Mexican wrestling."

crurotrichosis /KREW ro trik O sis/ n ● Excessive leg hair.

"As a pop-music diva, Bettina had an image to uphold, and her budget for personal upkeep would have maintained a fleet of ambulances. Not content with the usual retinue of hairstylist, nutritionist, manicurist, and the like, she also had a full-time staffer whose sole duty was to wage war on her chronic **crurotrichosis.**"

compare **pogogniasis**

cully /KULL ee/ n ● Someone who is easily imposed upon, especially by a woman.

"Julie liked to call the shots in a relationship, and she hated to be alone. But she always became bored with a man quickly, and so was always on the lookout for new prospective **cullies**."

compare **dictatrix**

CRUROTRICHOSIS

cumberworld /KUM ber world/ n ● 1) A person so deformed, lazy, or infirm as to be a burden to society. 2) A thoroughly useless person or thing.

"The culture critics argued that things had reached their all-time low, and who could disagree? Proof was the unparalleled success of the recent TV phenomenon, *Can You Be a* **Cumberworld?,** in which contestants sat around in a sumptuously decorated apartment and each tried to be even more thoroughly useless than the others."

∙ D ∙

dammarel /*DAM er el*/ n ● An effeminate man who spends all his time entertaining or courting women, and who is disinclined to the company of his own sex.

What a wonderfully specific word. It opens one's eyes to an entire class of men, and to the wonder that is the English language. Certainly **dammarels** must exist in other cultures, but how many tongues have a word for them?

"Woodburn the **dammarel** didn't exactly distinguish himself in The Big One. Rejected by the nursing corps and drafted into the infantry instead, he went AWOL and spent the rest of the war riveting battleships in drag."

compare **badling**

dandilly /*dan DILL ee*/ n ● A vain and spoiled woman.

Dandilly is something of a rarity, as there seem to be more words for vain males (*fop*, *dandy*, etc.) than for vain females in the English language. Could it be that once upon a time this vice was considered more disgraceful in a man than in a woman? And if so, why has this changed to the point where pectoral implants for men are now considered acceptable?

compare muscod

deadhead /DED *hed*/ n ● One who rides for free; a passenger who is not required to pay a fare.

The difference between a **deadhead** and a stowaway is that a **deadhead** does not have to hide while he siphons free rides on various conveyances. Hopefully, this excellent term will soon begin to shake loose of its musical groupie reference, and we can all go back to using **deadhead** the way it was intended.

"Bad enough that Becky's **deadhead** cousin had to cram the trunk with his guitar, forcing the other passengers to hold their bags on their laps. And that he subsisted on a type of fermented tofu, the odor of which seemed to emanate from his unwashed pores. But Justin also seemed to feel that since he wasn't contributing one penny toward gas or tolls, he was absolved from any responsibility to help fix the flat tire in the rain."

compare spunger

debacchate /DEB *uh kate*/ v ● To rage in the manner of one who has drunk overmuch of liquor.

"The wedding was marred slightly by the appearance of the bride's uncle, brandishing a champagne bottle and **debacchating** that he was going to kill the man who had stolen the honor of 'his little tulip.' "

compare barlichood

demivierge /*DEM ee vee airj*/ n ● A woman who is sexually promiscuous but retains her virginity.

While the authors can see nothing whatsoever that is insulting about this amazingly specific word, the definition is so delicious that we included it anyway.

To a handsome young buck named Serge
said Marge, who was feeling the urge,
"I'll give you some pleasure
but only a measure
*and remain a **demivierge**."*

compare **hogminny**

desticate /*DESS tik ate*/ v ● To cry out like a rat.

"Jonathon **desticated** in a horrid and pitiable manner, but the other boys involved in the teen prank gone awry all turned tail at the first sound of sirens, leaving him stuck halfway in the casement window."

compare **fream**

diamerdis /*die uh MURD iss*/ n ● A man who is covered in feces.

"Not only had the train ride to Paris taken sixteen hours, but Ernesto had been forced to share a small car with a subnormal **diamerdis** who insisted on sharing his cheese with him."

compare **imbulbitate, odorivector, stinkard**

dictatrix /*dik TAY trix*/ n ● A female dictator; a woman who tells people what to do.

"Exercising his own will had never been a passion for

William, so he settled down with a terrible **dictatrix** named Rhonda, and soon reported that he had never been happier."

compare **cully**

dietairistriae /DIE ter ISS tree ay/ n,pl • Women who go to female prostitutes.

Wait a second. Men who patronize ladies of the evening earn the humdrum moniker of *john*, while female customers warrant the elegant appellation of **dietairistriae?** What exactly is going on here?

compare **proxenetism**

dioestrum /die ESS trum/ n • A period of sexual inactivity between heats.

"His friends all laughed at his credulity, but Josh believed his girlfriend whenever she told him that she was 'having a **dioestrum** at the moment.' Although he did think it somewhat odd that she always chose to fill these times by taking her car to the burly mechanic's down the road for a tune-up."

dippoldism /DIP old ism/ n • The spanking or whipping of young children.

This term is derived from a sadistic German schoolteacher of yore named Dippold.

"At the recently opened School for Continuing Adult Education, the course in **dippoldism** being offered for the fall semester filled up almost at once. However, when it was revealed that the school was to hire a troupe of ill-tempered

DIPPOLDISM

midgets from the actor's union as stand-ins for the children, interest inexplicably waned."

compare comprachico

disseistrix /diss AY strix/ n ● A woman who separates someone from his or her possessions.

"The men lived in leaky houseboats and trailers off of red dirt roads. Most were alone; some had an old hound dog as a last friend from better days. They were hiding from the taxman, the lawman, and the repossessor. They were all victims of the **disseistrix,** and Josie's Roadside Tavern was the end of the line for most of them."

compare fogorner

dongon /DONG on/ n ● A person who is smart but appears stupid.

"Behind the glazed eyes, the slack jaw, and the stumbling speech, there actually lay an intelligent child, but Sherwin's teachers were all fooled by the little **dongon** and had long ago chalked him up as a lost cause."

draffsack /DRAFF sak/ n ● 1) A big paunch. 2) A lazy glutton.

Maybe this word does not possess the most exciting definitions, but it *is* insulting, and doesn't it dress up a page nicely? Originally, from a sack used to hold *draff,* meaning refuse.

"Her husband's huge **draffsack** didn't bother Mrs. Wong. She felt it lent him a certain . . . *substance,* and it also helped to keep other women at bay. She did wish that he wouldn't wear tight T-shirts in public quite so often, though."

driveler /*DRIV uh ler*/ n • One who slavers; one who talks in an idiotic fashion.

Most people are familiar with the word *drivel*, but few are aware that it exists in a form to describe an actual person. Since virtually everyone knows at least several **drivelers,** it behooves the authors to acquaint the general public with this word.

"He'd been warned that taking a bus trip across the entire country was a foolish idea at best, but Buford thought that it would be an interesting way to meet people. For two sleepless days and nights he sat scrunched next to a foul-smelling **driveler,** forced to listen to the man talk excitedly about his favorite sports biographies. Finally, he moved to the urine-soaked toilet at the back of the bus for the remainder of the trip."

compare **echolalia, naffin**

dunderwhelp /*DUN der welp*/ n • A detestable numbskull.

Many people live in a fantasy world, a bubble, if you will, from which they naively view our cerebrally challenged brethren with a sort of benign acceptance. They look upon the idiots of this world as kindly folk: a bit touched perhaps, but generally good at heart. They are wrong. Stupid people are put here to make life difficult and unpleasant for the rest of us, and it is high time we described these **dunderwhelps** with the contempt they deserve.

compare **knipperdollin, naffin**

dysmorphophiliac /*diss MORF o FEEL ee ak*/ n • A person with a preference for deformed sexual partners.

"It was well-known among the initiated that the ever-considerate Comtesse de Maude, consummate hostess that she was, kept a well-stocked stable of deformed sybarites, to ensure that the **dysmorphophiliacs** attending her orgies would never feel left out."

compare acrotophiliac

dyspareunia /*diss puh ROO nee uh*/ n ● Sex that is extremely difficult, uncomfortable, or painful.

Most people have experienced **dyspareunia** at some point in their lives. Whether it was that first time in a dark and cramped car, clumsily bumping various and sundry parts of anatomy with one's sweetheart—and becoming uncomfortably acquainted with the seat belt in the process—or the time when one's partner kept saying the wrong name.

"Too late did Jeff realize his folly in seeking to have his marriage annulled in the Texas courtroom by reason of **dyspareunia**. The preacher cum judge not only ruled against the plea, but also sternly admonished him that sex was only for the purpose of procreation, and not meant to be a pleasure."

compare apophallation, psychrotic

· E ·

echolalia /*ek o LAY lee uh*/ n ● Automatic and meaningless repetition of another's words and phrases.

While **echolalia** can be indicative of a mental disorder, it also crops up in people with nothing wrong with them other than that they are annoying.

"Larry's **echolalia** marked him as an imbecile. However, it also made him the perfect lackey for the schoolyard bully, and he could be seen tagging along after the ruffian all day, endlessly repeating his threats and insults. The two of them really made quite a pair."

compare **driveler**

ecomaniac /*eek o MAY nee AK*/ n ● One who is servile toward his boss but dictatorial toward his family.

"Simpering yes-man by day, swaggering bully by night—Sidney's **ecomania** caused him to be despised by two separate groups of people for two totally different reasons."

compare **fart-sucker, subsycophant**

egrote /*ee GROAT*/ v ● To feign sickness in order to avoid work.

Ah, to **egrote.** The question is: Is this a sin, a mark of defective character, or perhaps a sign of superior intelligence? Does the **egroter** have something that the rest of us sadly lack, and if so, how can we get it?

"Angus was always **egroting** his way out of all the unpleasant jobs at the garage. His deception finally caught up with him the day he met his demise on the oil-soaked floor, choking on a jelly doughnut as his coworkers ignored what they thought was yet another faked bout of gastrointestinal distress."

compare **lubbard, pathodixiac**

eisegetical /*eye zeh JET ik ul*/ adj ● Marked by a distorted explanation of text—especially Biblical text—to fit the meaning to preconceived notions.

"When Hazel found out that her husband had been taking the 'love thy neighbor' tenet to **eisegetical** lengths not mentioned in *her* Bible, she began spiking his coffee with a minute amount of drain clog remover each morning."

compare **antinomian, tartuffe**

emetomaniac /*em ET o MAY nee ak*/ n ● A person with an abnormal propensity to vomit frequently.

"With their bold promises and flashy advertising campaign ('Eat like a cow and still lose weight!!!'), the authors of *The Ruminant's Cookbook* made a fortune by tapping into a lucrative and largely unexplored vein of **emetomania** in the general public."

compare **bevomit, hyperemian**

empleomaniac */em PLEE o MAY nee ak/* n ● One who is overly eager to hold public office.

People who are overeager to hold public office obviously fall into one of three categories: 1) They are inherently corrupt and seek to make a fortune at the taxpayer's expense. 2) They are simpleminded or delusional enough to believe that they can actually "make a difference." 3) They are completely insane.

It doesn't matter which category they fall into; **empleomaniacs** should be immediately disqualified for any public office higher than school crossing guard.

compare **malversation**

engrease */en GREASE/* v ● To become fat.

"Gus loved being a short-order cook. The pop and sizzle of frying bacon, the buzz of hungry customers. Sadly, as a result of his thrifty yet ill-advised habit of ending each shift by eating all the griddle scraps with a side helping of liquid lard, he was **engreasing** at an alarming rate."

compare **lipophilic**

entheomaniac */en THEE o MAY nee ak/* n ● One who is literally insane about religion.

"Easter seemed to lose some of its carefree spirit for the children the year they celebrated it at the country home of their Aunt Helen, an **entheomaniac** who insisted that they recite an hour of the Scriptures before hunting for eggs. She ended the day with a lecture on what happens to children who go to Hell, illustrated nicely by microwaving a foil-wrapped chocolate bunny rabbit."

compare **tartuffe**

epicaricacy */ep ik AAH rik uh see/* n • Pleasure from the misfortunes of others.

An underutilized jewel. What a word! What a concept! It should bring joy to the hearts of all the people (the majority of the readers of this volume) who chuckle inwardly when they see someone trip and fall or step into a glistening pile of dog droppings.

Sadly, **epicaricacy** has been unfairly neglected over the years. Numerous modern English dictionaries make no mention of it; meanwhile, they see fit to include the German word *schadenfreude* (same definition), apparently for the sole reason that it fills a void in our language! The fact is, long before *schadenfreude* wormed its way into the lexicon, there existed an English word for the exact same concept. **Epicaricacy** has a noble lineage, coming from the Greek roots of *epi* (upon) + *chara* (joy) + *kakon* (evil). And it has appeared in many old and esteemed dictionaries. Yet the word is now largely ignored in favor of a foreign interloper.

"The residents of quiet, tree-lined Bowker Street were a peaceful lot as a rule, but their feathers got a bit ruffled when the local ice cream truck man refused to lower the volume of the horrid wheedling music his vehicle constantly emanated. And so when the deranged war veteran from the next block destroyed the truck with a bazooka one fine spring morning, they all felt the warm glow of **epicaricacy** spreading through their veins."

compare **ucalegon**

epigone */ep IG uh nee/* n • 1) An imitator born in a later generation. 2) An undistinguished follower of an accomplished master.

This can be a useful word and it makes an excellent underhanded insult. **Epigones** abound in many fields: the arts are one clear example. And so few people grasp the true meaning of this word, especially when slipped into everyday conversation, that if a candidate for higher office were to be introduced to the masses as "the **epigone** of a long line of American patriots," he would probably not lose many votes.

eproctolagniac /eh PROK toe LAG nee ak/ n • Someone who is sexually stimulated by flatulence, his own or someone else's.

Some men keep a porn collection under their bed for those occasions when they desire to be intimate with themselves. For the **eproctolagniac,** a jar of refried beans is more effective.

compare **aerocolpos, feist**

excerebrose /ex SEH reh brose/ adj • Brainless.

This word not only describes the Scarecrow from *The Wizard of Oz*, but a significant portion of humanity as well—and certainly the bulk of our cultural output. Do not confuse **excerebrose** with the remarkably similar *excerebrate* (to beat the brains out), although the one might very well prompt the other.

"As a producer, Rutman skyrocketed to moguldom behind a series of lowbrow comedies starring a lovable chimpanzee, each film being more **excerebrose** than the last."

compare **dunderwhelp**

exopthalmos /ex op THAL mose/ adj • Having protruding eyeballs; bug-eyed.

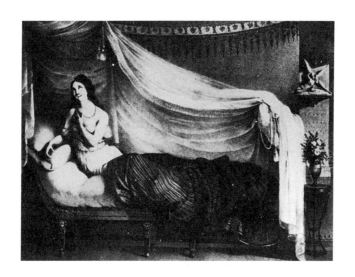

EPROCTOLAGNIAC

"Jerry, the hypertensive and **exopthalmos** middle manager who always needed things done yesterday, trod all over the secretarial pool for years. When he finally suffered a massive heart attack while trying to unjam the copy machine, all the ladies chipped in and purchased a large gilt frame to enshrine the offending piece of crinkled paper."

exsibilate /*ex SIB il ate*/ v ● To hiss off the stage.
For all the drama buffs out there: the only word that one really needs to know when discussing bad theater.
compare cantabank

eyeservant */EYE serv ent/* n ● One who works only when being watched.

Everyone has a little bit of **eyeservant** in them. Face it: The only thing that keeps most of us working at our jobs is the fear of being found out if we don't. Those who can coast, do.

"Starting and stopping so many times took almost as much energy as working the whole day through, but Wilson was a proud and practiced **eyeservant,** gifted with astounding peripheral vision, and without a foreman looking in his direction, he wouldn't dig."

compare **aidle, ploiter**

· F ·

fabiform */FAB if orm/* adj ● Shaped like a bean.

Fabiform cuts to the quick of what this book is all about: providing the most specific and exact term to correctly insult every person one might possibly encounter. No matter how well versed one is in the art of vulgarity, one can always use a word that will slice through a target's defenses, precisely summing up their flaws to the extent that they feel truly horrible about themselves. **Fabiform** is such a word.

Granted, "shaped like a bean" is not a concept that immediately evokes images of grown men breaking down and crying upon hearing themselves thus described. But if one takes a moment to picture in one's mind a kidney bean, with its distinctive curvature, and then adds a set of arms, legs, and a head to it, an image coalesces of a swaybacked sort of man, his stomach protruding a full twelve inches in front of where his skinny shoulders are: a **fabiform** man.

fanaticise */fan AT iss ize/* v ● To behave like a fanatic.

Fanatic is a common word for an all-too-common type of

individual. But most people are unaware that it exists as a verb as well.

"Luther **fanaticised** over his diet and the diets of those around him incessantly, straining his leafy green vegetables every night before going to bed and constantly upbraiding his roommates over their caloric intake. One day when they could take no more, they tied him to a chair and force-fed him pickled herring until he wept."

compare **knipperdollin**

fart-sucker /FART suk er/ n ● A brown-noser; one who sucks up to superiors.

"Pettiford didn't mind running errands for his boss; it was a surefire way to climb the corporate ladder. And while it also didn't bother him when he became known within the firm as the 'little **fart-sucker**,' he did wish his coworkers would at least stick to his official title in company memos."

compare **ecomaniac, subsycophant**

feculent /FEK yoo lent/ adj ● Covered in feces.

The world would probably be a happier place if we never had need for a word like **feculent**. Unfortunately, situations calling for its use are more common than one might at first believe. It might even have a place in negative restaurant reviews—used metaphorically, of course.

"Trying out his new Rollerblades for the first time, Fullerton brought his mastiff down to the overused dog run in the park after a rainstorm. He was so horridly **feculent** when he finally made it back home that his doorman wouldn't let him into the building without first hosing him off on the sidewalk."

compare **bedung, diamerdis**

feist /FEIST/ n ● A silent fart.

Why is this word not included in dictionaries of today? It is a major instance of modern lexicography gone awry. **Feist** is exactly the sort of word that would prick up the ears of any thirteen-year-old, doing wonders to spark a more-than-superficial interest in our language. Perhaps *that's* why. . . .

"The disgusting and flatulent little toad from Word Processing was forever in the habit of letting loose with **feists** while lunching in the company cafeteria, and would always give himself away by tittering loudly when he did so."

compare **eproctolagniac**

fico /FIKE o/ n ● A gesture, thrusting the thumb between the middle and forefinger of a closed fist, that is indicative of deep contempt.

While this word is not terribly insulting in and of itself, it does have a romantic and insulting pedigree.

Let us go back in time to strife-torn twelfth-century Europe. Our story centers on Frederick Barbarossa, a German prince who captured Milan in the 1160s, but was expelled a short time later. While removing him from their city, the Milanese took occasion to humiliate Barbarossa's wife in a manner unspecified by accounts of the period. He was not a man to look kindly upon such a deed (whatever it was), so when he retook Milan he exacted a strange and horrific revenge.

He began by having every able-bodied man of the city kneel behind the posterior of a defecating mule. As the mule voided what he had to void, the poor man behind it was forced, on pain of death, to take the lump of excrement between his teeth and, turning to his captors, say, "Ecco la fica" ("Behold the fig").

Although the physical gesture in question has been around since time immemorial, only after Freddy Barbarossa did it assume the meaning that it has today. He truly was the father of the **fico**, and in this respect he was a visionary.

fireship /*FIRE ship*/ n • A diseased prostitute.

A very special and very troubling word. While we are by no means seeking to cast judgment on prostitution (patrons or purveyors), a diseased prostitute is a fairly unappetizing notion by any measure.

" 'Boss Fats' McKenzie was no do-gooder, and preferred to be a hands-off mayor, but when the spread of **fireships** threatened his town's lucrative prostitution trade, he leapt into action quicker than the Sisters of Mercy at a church picnic struck by lightning."

compare **frenchified**

fissilingual /*FISS il ING wool*/ adj • Possessing a forked tongue.

"Staring out at his barren window box, Boddington cursed

that **fissilingual** convenience-store owner. He should never have agreed to trade his winning lottery ticket for a pouch of 'magic beans.' "

compare abydocomist

fogorner /FOG or ner/ n ● Formerly, a person whose job it was to expel people from their residences.

"Patsy just loved working as a **fogorner.** The shocked looks on the families' faces when she served the eviction notices, the wails and piteous cries of the indignant, and most of all, the feeling that she was really accomplishing something. Why, it made her feel all proud inside."

compare disseistrix

foveated /FO vee ate ed/ adj ● Covered with little pits, such as those left from smallpox.

Apart from golf balls and English muffins, few things improve from being **foveated.**

"Bad enough that Wayne had broken out in a terrible case of acne on the eve of the prom, but his do-it-yourself remedy with household bleach and a turkey baster left his face more **foveated** than a brick of baby Swiss cheese."

fream /FREEM/ v ● To roar like a wild boar during the rutting season, when he seeks to mate.

"Douglaston continued his nightly ritual of adding to an already porcine physique with a diet of low-grade beer and stale bar pretzels. And although he was practically **freaming** at every woman who entered the bar, not one of them ever showed the slightest inclination to go outside and rut with him in his minivan."

compare strene

frenchified /FRENCH if ide/ adj ● 1) To have contracted a venereal disease. 2) To have become like the French.

Most people are aware of the second definition of this adjective, but not the first (although it is a toss-up as to which of the twain is more insulting). One must really give credit for this word where credit is due; namely to the English and their peculiar blend of humor, disdain, and good old-fashioned xenophobia.

"Lisa Hickstrom's parents breathed a sigh of relief. The news sounded good: Their formerly wayward teen daughter was becoming 'thoroughly **frenchified**' in Paris on the study-abroad program. Apparently a change of scenery was just what the young hellion needed."

compare fireship, ranivorous

furfuraceous /FUR fur AY shuss/ adj ● Covered in dandruff; afflicted with dandruff.

"Young Jennifer had just moved to the big city from the suburbs, and so much wanted to become one of the 'in' crowd that she would always dress completely in black. The problem was, she was so **furfuraceous** that she had to discreetly carry a little whisk brush with her at all times."

fustilarian /FYOOST il AIR ee an/ n ● One who pursues worthless objects or aims.

That this word describes almost all of us is one bleak

observation. Not to be preachy, but **fustilarian** certainly provides food for thought, because what a person sees as worthless depends on what a person values: A greedy fellow who only cares for money might consider someone who pursues love to be a **fustilarian**.

compare **nihilarian**

· G ·

gammerstang /*GAM er stang*/ n ● A tall, skinny, and awkward woman.

"Who could have predicted that the shy young **gammerstang,** forever bumping her head on doorways and blushing in company, would blossom into a gorgeous and successful runway model? Or that she would soon metamorphose again, this time into a pill-popping, anorexic prima donna?"

compare **scrag**

gandermooner /*GAND er moon er*/ n ● A man who chases women during the month after his wife has given birth.

This is an amazingly specific word. A **gandermooner** is not just a man who cheats on his wife, but one who cheats on his wife during a very narrow window of opportunity. It raises a question: When was this phenomenon so pronounced as to have warranted a special term?

"Some of the regulars in the pub liked to reminisce about their honeymoons, but not old Mr. McGillicuddy. The old **gandermooner's** chief source of delight lay in reliving the many escapades he had enjoyed as the father of twelve—and in cursing his twins for 'cheating' him out of yet another one."

compare liffy

gaucy /*GOSS ee*/ adj • Fat and comely.

Note that a person so described is unlikely to overflow with gratitude. Half insult and half compliment, **gaucy** is useful when one wishes to deprecate someone in the nicest way possible.

> *This girl I once knew was the heights—*
> *nay, the acme of fleshy delights.*
> *Sweet-faced and **gaucy**,*
> *my trollop so saucy,*
> *I miss her on cold winter nights.*

geromorphic /*jer o MORF ik*/ adj • Prematurely aged; appearing older than one is.

In today's youth-obsessed culture, being **geromorphic** is a fate worse than death. But as strange as it may sound, in certain long-forgotten periods of history old people were actually respected and admired. At those times, **geomorphism** had a silver lining, as it does today for underage drinkers.

"At first Liz's new classmates shunned the unlucky girl with the lined, leathery skin and graying hair. But after she demonstrated her ability to put her **geromorphism** to good use procuring wine coolers, she became very popular on Friday and Saturday nights."

compare raddled

gink /GINK/ n • An insignificant person.

"At their tenth high school reunion, all of the former cheerleaders and football players were quietly outraged that the class **gink,** whom almost no one remembered at all, had gone on to become a computer mogul of enormous wealth. At their twentieth reunion, they were all secretly pleased with the news that he had died of an aneurysm the previous spring."

glouping /GLAU ping/ adj • Dumb and sullen.

The word **glouping** somehow just *looks* dumb and sullen. Anyone who has been on a rainy camping trip with young children should be familiar with its meaning.

glump /GLUMP/ n • A sulking crank.

"Old Mr. Kemp truly hated children, and cultivated his reputation as the town **glump** by sitting on a park bench all day long, spitting bits and pieces of wet popcorn at the mothers who passed by with their strollers."

gobemouche /go beh MOOSH/ n • A gullible person.

Deriving from the French (literally "swallow-fly"; i.e., one who will swallow anything), **gobemouche** is a nice, memorable little term for a credulous person.

"The sweepstakes people had unearthed a true **gobemouche** in Cassandra. Every time she got a piece of junk mail telling her she had 'already won a million dollars,' she hopped on a plane and flew down to their headquarters to pick up her nonexistent winnings."

GLOUPING

goller /GOLL er/ v • To utter loud and unintelligible gurgling noises, especially when shouting in rage.

This happens rather frequently with enraged people and is usually quite funny to watch—from a distance. What red-blooded child doesn't enjoy provoking a substitute teacher or some other adult victim to the point where he or she starts to **goller?**

"As Glanders watched his new seventy-five-foot yacht being bashed to and fro in the marina with his idiot son-in-law at the controls, he could do nothing but stand at the end of the dock, **gollering** in impotent fury."

compare aggramaticist

gongoozler /gon GOOZ ler/ n • A dimwit who stares at unusual things.

The term **gongoozler** was formerly applied to a type of lowlife who hung out of windows and gaped at passersby. In certain neighborhoods this creature is still alive and well today. However, the authors suggest extending the word to include, say, people who stare out of the windows of automobiles. Imagine the traffic reporter saying, "We have fifteen-minute delays on the George Washington Bridge, where traffic is all backed up due to a three-car accident and **gongoozling** in the left lane. . . ."

grimalkin /grim ALL kin/ n • A jealous or imperious old woman.

[*gray* + *malkin* mop, scarecrow, kitchen maid, or cat]

Grimalkin is a pretty nasty word to call a woman, perfect for occasions that call for the strongest form of verbal abuse.

"Cindy knew the spiteful old **grimalkins** on the parole board would never have mercy on *her*—a young and gorgeous game-show hostess who had it all but got mixed up in the dangerous world of tropical-fish smuggling. She concentrated instead on plans for escape."

compare twitchel

grimthorpe /GRIM *thorp*/ v ● To do a rotten job of restoration.

So called after Sir Edmund Beckett, the first Baron Grimthorpe, an architect who was severely criticized for his botched restoration of St. Albans Cathedral in England.

"When the refuse from the toilet began flowing from the kitchen faucets, it became clear to us that our house had been **grimthorped** in the worst possible way."

compare antivitruvian

grizely /GRIZ *uh lee*/ adj ● Extraordinarily ugly.

Thanks in large part to modern architecture, new words for "extremely ugly" are always in demand. And while saying that something "looks like shit" will always get the point across, the reader may find it marginally empowering to have **grizely** at his disposal, even if he would really prefer a wrecking ball.

"Dominick, the high-strung and aesthetically snobbish interior decorator, recoiled in horror from his community service assignment. For shoplifting designer scarves, he was sentenced to helping seniors craft **grizely** mobiles out of shrinky-dinks and dried macaroni; he wished he'd been sentenced to jail instead."

gubbertush */GUB er tush/* n ⬤ A bucktoothed person.

"Once a year for an entire week in August the towns-people would line up and cheer on Belvedere, the scrawny, tow-headed little **gubbertush**, as he defeated all comers in the county-wide corn-eating contest. Effortlessly sawing row after row of kernels into his mouth, for those few days he was their hometown pride."

compare brochity

gulchin */GULL chin/* n ⬤ A little or young glutton.

"It was always good sport to tease and steal the lunch of Harvey, the rotund **gulchin** in the fourth grade, but it was almost too easy. He wept at the drop of a hat, and besides, he was far too portly to chase anybody very far."

compare barathrum

gundygut */GUN dee gut/* n ⬤ An offensive, mannerless eater.

This is a fine term of somewhat jocular abuse, good among other things for hammering home table manners to small children: "Take human bites, you **gundyguts!**"

"Whenever Sheryl wanted to shed a couple of pounds, she would wait until twelve o'clock and peer over the cubicle wall at her coworker with the muttonchop sideburns. Watching that **gundygut** stuff his face invariably put her off her lunch."

compare slotterhodge

· H ·

hippomanic /hip o MAN ik/ adj • Lusting after horses.

"Geoffrey Vanderbern was the most renowned polo player in the district, due largely to the uncanny rapport he shared with Platypus, his faithful mount. When a meddling scandalmonger threatened to expose him as a **hippomanic** deviant, it cost him two of his country houses to have the story quashed."

compare **avisodomy**

hirquiticke /her KWIT ik/ n • "One past foureteene yeeres of age, beginning to bee moved with venus delight" (Cockeram's *English Dictionarie* of 1623).

Most people look back on this tender and vulnerable stage of awakening sexuality with a certain nostalgia, tempered by an overwhelming relief that they never have to go through it again.

compare **demivierge**

HOGMINNY

hogminny /hog MIN ee/ n • A depraved young woman.

Just like beauty, that which is insulting is entirely in the eye of the beholder.

"Nursing their hot toddies on cold autumn nights, the lads in the tavern loved to hoist their robust voices in song. And none of their ditties ever brought more tears to more eyes than that wistful ode, *Winnie My **Hogminny**.*"

compare **parepithymia**

hybristophiliac /hib RIST o FEEL ee ak/ n ● One who becomes sexually aroused from being with a violent criminal.

In spite of the inherent danger involved (or perhaps because of it), **hybristophiliacs** are doing their part to ensure that the Evil Gene gets passed down to the next generation.

"Dedicated to discreetly servicing **hybristophiliac** women with means, www.dateafelon.com quickly grew from a small Internet start-up into a cyber cash cow."

hygeiolatry /hi jee OLL uh tree/ n ● Health fanaticism.

This word is more useful today than ever, for even as the population as a whole grows more obese and sickly, a lunatic fringe errs in the other direction. These odd and pathetic creatures are easily identified not by their aversion to steak, cheese, and all the other things that generally make life worth living, but by their hysterical opposition to anyone who seems to be enjoying himself.

"The frequent ice-cold plunge baths, the rolfings, the all-squid diet . . . it was all part and parcel of Marlon's **hygeiolatry**—as were the sunken cheeks, the greenish complexion, and the disagreeable body odor."

compare **fanaticise, knipperdollin**

hyperemian /hype er EE mee an/ n ● One who vomits excessively.

[Greek *hyper* above + *emesis* vomiting]

"Stuck for a name for their new multimillion-dollar backwards and upside-down roller coaster, amusement park officials considered dozens of choices before finally settling on 'The **Hyperemian.**' "

compare **bevomit, emetomaniac**

hypobulic /hype o BOOL ik/ adj ● Unable to make decisions.

[Greek *hypo* under + *boule* will]

Paper or plastic? Chocolate or vanilla? Choice is a precious aspect of freedom, but to the **hypobulic** soul it can paradoxically be quite oppressive. If only they would repeat to themselves the following mantra: "It doesn't matter!"

hypomaniac /hype o MAY nee ak/ n ● A person with a mental disturbance characterized by excessive optimism.

[Greek *hypo* under + *mania* madness]

Supreme confidence, or **hypomania**? The line between the two is sometimes a fine one indeed. Take for example the prefight interview in which the unknown boxer about to be pulverized by the champion speaks hopefully about "fighting his fight" and so forth. Three minutes later, spitting out broken teeth, he says the ref stopped the match too soon. What is one to do with such people—admire them for their unconquerable spirit, or condemn them for their stupidity? Perhaps both.

compare **macromaniac**

imbonity /*im BON it ee*/ n • The absence of good qualities.

[Late Latin *imbonitas* evil condition]

Applicable to both persons and things, **imbonity** says it all. Consider the airplane meal that is late arriving, cold, tasteless, fattening, *and* too small. Or the Hollywood movie that is not only boring and offensive but over three hours long as well. These are all-too-common examples of modern-day **imbonity.**

compare **shilpit**

imbulbitate /*im BULB it ate*/ v • To defecate in one's pants.

[Latin *imbulbitare* to befoul, defile]

There really is no tiptoeing around the definition of this word.

" 'Oh, No!' " said Roscoe, as he tried in vain to extricate himself from between the elevator doors. '**Imbulbitated** again!' "

compare **alacuoth, diamerdis**

infandous */IN fan duss/* adj ● Too odious to be spoken of.

[Latin *infandus* unspeakable]

Why is this word not more widely known? Perhaps because in this day and age there is simply *nothing* too odious to be splashed across a front page or made into a TV special, let alone spoken of. **Infandous** is a quaint old term hearkening back to a time when people actually knew shame.

The noun form of the word is **infandum.**

"J. Ackleby liked to sit back and ruminate over the many **infandous** stunts he'd pulled over the course of a long and fruitful career in publicity. It always brought a smile to his face to think of the time he'd entered the Siamese twins in the doubles open Ping-Pong tournament."

infausting */n FOSS ting/* adj ● Inflicting bad luck upon others.

[Latin *infaustus* unfortunate]

"Craig loved taking his buddies out fishing in his boat, but whenever his pushy brother-in-law insisted on coming along no one caught any fish. One hot Sunday afternoon the men finally snapped, stranding the **infausting** fellow on a buoy with nothing but a bag of minnows and a transistor radio running low on batteries."

ingler */ING ler/* n ● The passive participant in anal intercourse.

A versatile word, **ingler** can be either a mortal insult or a term of endearment, depending upon one's milieu.

compare **poger, sodomitess**

inkle /INK l/ v ● To attend a party to which one has not been invited.

Sir Leslie so needed to tinkle
*that he soon attempted to **inkle***
a gala soiree
that turned him away,
so their hedgerows he did sprinkle.

insiliarius /in SIL ee AIR ee us/ n ● An evil advisor.

This saboteur is usually hard to spot until after his or her damage is done, but can be useful once identified; just do the opposite of what he or she recommends.

"After he attempted to impress his beloved by lifting the dung cart—with disastrous results—Amos realized that as far as winning his heart's desire was concerned, his brother was an **insiliarius** whose advice was to be disregarded at all costs."

compare **leguleian**

J

jehu /*JAY hoo*/ n • A reckless driver.

In ancient times, **Jehu** was a king of Israel known for his furious and daring chariot attacks. In modern parlance, this eponymous word denotes someone who should have his or her driver's license revoked.

"Veronica frequently found her eccentric stepfather to be a source of great embarrassment, and never more so than when he would drop her off at her high school. Often while she made her way through the parking lot to the front steps, he would lean out of his driver's side window, shaking his fist with rage at students who drove their own cars with what he decided was reckless abandon: "Damn you, you young jackanapes! You **jehus!**"

jobberknowle /*JOB er nowl*/ n • A heavy and dim-witted person.

It sounds rather like some fabulous creature out of nineteenth-century children's fiction, but alas, the **jobberknowle** is about as ethereal as a tollbooth clerk. If the reader wishes to see one, all he or she has to do is call the phone company and ask to have another line installed; they'll send one right over.

compare **looby**

· K ·

kakopygian /*kak o PIE gee an*/ adj　●　Possessing an ugly set of buttocks.

[Greek *kakos* bad + *pyge* rump]

In *Depraved English*, the authors brought to light words for nice asses, fat asses, and hairy asses, not taking into account the overlap among these terms. After all, some people think that fat asses are nice, and there may even be some who are fond of hairy asses. In the interest of fairness, **kakopygian** is offered for anyone with a need to express his or her displeasure with someone's posterior.

"Jurgen Wallace had always been ahead of his time as a choreographer; some even called him a visionary. But the debut of his latest opus, 'The **Kakopygian's** Waddle,' ended in disaster when those members of the audience who did not flee in disgust charged the stage howling with fury, forcing his entire troupe to scurry to safety as best they could."

compare **apoglutic, unipygic**

kedge /KEJ/ v ● To fill oneself with meat.

Kedge is not a particularly insulting word, but it certainly is unpleasant.

"Preston just could not pass up a bet involving food. As a result, he was now so thoroughly **kedged** that he could not leave the steak house under his own power, and was restricted to a vocabulary of grunts and moans."

klazomaniac /klaz o MAY nee ak/ n ● A compulsive shouter; one who speaks entirely in shouts.

Whenever sharing space with a **klazomaniac** is unavoidable, it is best not to exercise any restraint in making your displeasure known. There is no reason why anyone, even if he is stone deaf, should yell directly and incessantly into your face. The idiot probably just loves the sound of his or her own voice.

compare **cachinnator**

klismaphiliac /kliz muh FEEL ee ak/ n ● A person with a sexual interest in receiving enemas.

King Louis XIV of France deserves special mention in any discussion of enemas. While it is not known if he obtained sexual gratification through the practice, he certainly took his irrigation seriously. He even had a special throne built so that he might continue with his cleansing while attending to matters of state. According to the written records of the time, he submitted to these internal ablutions more than two thousand times during his reign.

"Too ashamed to admit to anyone that he was a **klisma-philiac,** Mallory would go to absurd lengths to justify garnering himself an enema, often by consuming vast quantities of a homemade concoction of system-blocking foods mixed with sawdust."

knipperdollin */nip er DOLL in/* n • A fanatical idiot.
[From Bernhard Knipperdolling, fanatical leader of the Munster Anabaptists from 1533 to 1535]

This is a surprisingly useful word for what is potentially a very dangerous person. Although a case can be made that a fanatical idiot is less threatening than a clever one, are not all fanatics idiotic to some extent? This much is for sure: When confronted with a **knipperdollin,** there is no middle ground. One must either flee immediately, or send him off on a suicide mission posthaste.

compare **fanaticise, naffin**

· L ·

legruita /*LEG roo EET uh*/ n ● A fine or penalty for undue familiarity with a woman.

"It became an infamous scam: Whenever the town's coffers ran low, the wily Marshal Blackstone would set out a string of well-baited **legruita** traps. It was never very long before much-needed revenue began pouring in."

leguleian /*leg YOOL ee an*/ n ● A small-time lawyer. adj ● Resembling a lawyer.

[Latin *leguleius* a pettifogging lawyer]

This word more than fulfills the criteria of an insult, in either its primary or secondary sense.

"With the sweat pouring off of him in the midday sun, Milton's bewildered father vowed that he would never again fall victim to one of his precocious son's **leguleian** tricks for getting out of mowing the lawn."

compare **barrator, bdelloid, rabulistic**

LEINT

leint /*LAINT*/ v • To add urine to ale to make it stronger.

More than modern dentistry, or even the abolition of debtors' prison, this appalling practice illustrates why it is better to be alive today than in the eighteenth century: We no longer feel the need to piss in our beer.

" 'Would you like something stronger to go with that?' the bartender asked the troubled salesman while drawing his ale from the tap. 'No,' came the reply. 'I'm off the rum tonight; just make sure you **leint** that pint before you serve it.' "

compare **uriposiac**

lickspigot /*LIK spig ot*/ n • A revolting parasite.
*The **lickspigot** lay anxious in wait*
for the diners to finish their date.

Their departure was sped
when he came up and said,
"Do you mind if I lick off your plate?"
          compare **fart-sucker, scaff**

licktwat /*LIK twat*/ n • A term of contempt.

A word of genuine mystery, **licktwat** appears in numerous dictionaries but is never defined. Lexicographers seem content to list the word alone, trusting either to the inherent knowledge or the salacious imagination of their readers. Lacking an authoritative source, the authors are reluctant to assign it a specific meaning, and will list it only as a general term of opprobrium.

Of course, following the example set by numerous other words (**lickspigot,** *lickpenny*, etc.), one may safely assume that this word is not only a term of contempt, but a remarkably naughty one as well. Such words give the lie to the fallacious argument that the once-dignified English tongue is rapidly vulgarizing, for **licktwat** and many other terms just as salty are hundreds of years old. English is a filthy language, and always has been.

An interesting aside on the word *twat*: In a fairly infamous literary faux pas, Robert Browning once mistakenly used the word in a poem to refer to part of a nun's outfit. He made the error after reading this passage from *Vanity of Vanities* from 1660: "They talk't of his having a Cardinall's hat, They'd send him as soon an Old Nun's Twat."
          compare **tittery-whoppet**

liffy /*LIFF ee*/ v • To seduce a woman with promises of fidelity, and then desert her.

"George wanted nothing so much as to be able to **liffy** every woman that he met. He was thwarted in his efforts, however, as even those few that he did succeed in bedding summarily dumped him immediately afterward."

Ed's fancy being smitten
by a saucy pert young kitten,
he wooed her on the phone
and dodged her chaperone.

After deflowering his dame,
Ed soon tired of the game.
His conscience being iffy,
he decided he would **liffy**
and try his luck again.

compare **legruita**

limberham /*LIM ber ham*/ n • An obsequious, servile person.

Who needs yoga? The **limberham** is supple-jointed from bowing and scraping.

"Sanford's waiter turned out to be such a simpering **limberham** that it made him feel profoundly uncomfortable. Halfway through his dinner he saw no alternative but to begin abusing him terribly—anything to stop that horrible fawning."

compare **fart-sucker, timeserver**

limitarian /*lim it AIR ee an*/ n • One who believes that salvation is restricted to a certain group of individuals.

LIFFY

These self-righteous religious exclusionists have caused a lot of trouble over the centuries. Maybe there ought to be a special section reserved for them in Hell.

compare **antinomian**

lipophilic /*lip o FILL ik*/ adj ● Having an affinity for fat.
[Greek *lipos* fat + *philein* to love]

Although this is a medical term, **lipophilic** may have uses above and beyond those it has heretofore known. Specifically, it could be applied to those people who demonstrate a proclivity for members of the opposite sex who can only be described as obese.

"Most of his fellow construction workers also favored women of above-average heft, but the **lipophilic** Louis would grunt excitedly at only the most corpulent specimens of femininity, and, staring at their posteriors as they walked by, exclaim, 'Unh! Baby! It looks like two ten-years-olds fighting under a blanket!' "

compare **engrease**

looby /*LOO bee*/ n ● An awkward, unwieldy oaf; often stupid and lazy as well.

" 'Well I'll be,' drawled Willie's gym teacher, pointing up at the terrified teen. 'That **looby** on the knotted rope is funnier-lookin' than a monkey tryin' to fuck a greased football! Let's keep 'im up there!' "

compare **jobberknowle**

lubbard /*LUB ard*/ n ● An idle fellow; a man who could work, but doesn't.

LUBBARD

[Middle English *lobre* a fat lazy fellow]

"Being profiled in ***Lubbard's Life*** magazine filled Maxwell with a sense of pride: the same kind he got from a job well shirked. There he was on the cover, big as life, grinning as he posed outside his home—grandpa's toolshed—under the caption 'It takes a real man not to work.' "

compare **egrote**

· M ·

mab /*MAB*/ v ● To dress oneself in a careless manner.

"For the third time in a week, Lindsey slept right through his alarm clock. Now he had just enough time to splash his face, **mab,** and dash off to catch the crowded train to work. Squeezing into the car just as the doors closed, he beheld a sea of silent staring faces, which alerted him to the fact that he had no pants on."

compare **bedizen**

macromaniac /*MAK ro MAY nee ak*/ n ● One under the delusion that a part of his or her body is larger than it actually is.

[Greek *makros* long + *mania* madness]

"An incurable **macromaniac,** J. C. was never bothered by the peals of feminine laughter that accompanied his every striptease. And with all the sympathy tips he collected from patrons who took pity on him, he wound up earning more than any other male exotic dancer in the club."

compare **brachyphallic**

MAB

malversation /*mal ver ZAY shun*/ n ● Corruption in office; misuse of public funds.

"The citizens at the town meeting bristled with indignation when it was revealed that the bulk of the newly uncovered **malversation** had gone toward providing psychological counseling for the mayor's three spoiled children, in the wake of the episode when they set the mailman's truck on fire."

compare **empleomaniac**

mangonist /*MAN gon ist*/ n ● One who dresses up inferior wares for sale.

"Spit and elbow grease were fine for all those mom-and-pop-type antique stores that sold heirloom silver, but Emilio the **mangonist** found that painting his wares with a pewter-like gloss and issuing seals of authenticity worked just as well."

compare **comprachico, grimthorpe**

maritality /*ma rih TAL it ee*/ n ● Excessive fondness for one's husband.

"With the knowledge that she gleaned from her week at the self-awareness seminar, Joy returned home with a steely resolve not to give her undeserving husband the **maritality** he had come to expect. Instead, she would dote on her shih tzu."

compare **mariturient**

mariturient /*ma rih TYOO ree ent*/ adj ● Desiring to become a husband.

There is nothing wrong with being just a bit **mariturient.**

MANGONIST

But any quality, no matter how sterling it might be, can be taken to unreasonable lengths.

"**Mariturient** at any cost, Lincoln displayed a desperation that paid dividends of misery in the long run. His shrewish bride knew from the start that she was doing him a tremendous favor by marrying him, and she never let him forget it."

compare **maritality**

marplot /MAR plot/ n • A person who interferes; one who ruins the best-laid plans.

"The wrestling team at Northanger High wasn't pleased to have their closed-door locker-room romps exposed to the rest of the school, and thus few were surprised when they grabbed the **marplot** from the student newspaper, wrapped him head to toe in adhesive tape, and stuck him in a rather small locker, forgetting that a long weekend was coming up."

martext /MAR text/ n • A blundering preacher.

"The **martext** presiding at the wedding arrived late and drunk, lost his place several times during his rambling speech, and needed to be propped up by a groomsman. Just when it seemed like things couldn't get any worse, he called the bride by the wrong name during the exchange of vows, and it began to look like Julian would never get to marry his high school sweetheart after all."

mattoid /MAT oid/ n • A semi-insane person.
[Latin *mattus* stupid, drunk]
A word for a semi-insane person is long overdue. **Mattoid**

comes to us via the medical profession, where it refers to a specific diagnosis. Might it not be better used to describe those people who have something odd about them that one can't quite put one's finger on (until a switch gets thrown and they go bananas)?

"The fur muffler worn in July should have been a tip-off, but Brenda was feeling frisky, so she struck up a conversation with the **mattoid** sitting next to her on the train. It soon became evident that this had been a serious error in judgment."

compare **crackheaded**

meretriculate /*meh ruh TRIK yoo late*/ v ● To deceive, as does a whore.

How exactly does a whore deceive? It might be in any one of a number of ways. She (or he) could pretend to be of a different sex, for example, or welsh on a payment made in advance. Presumably, a whore might even represent herself or himself as having greater sexual prowess than is in fact the case. In any event, since the authors unfortunately do not have information at their disposal to further elucidate this verb and are sorely lacking in personal experience in this area, readers are advised to use **meretriculate** as best they see fit, to describe the actions of various species, male or female, that they disapprove of.

compare **chrematisophiliac**

micropenis /*MIKE ro PEE niss*/ n ● A penis that is less than two centimeters long.

There are many words in the English language for small

penises—and those endowed with them. **Micropenis** stands out (or doesn't stand out) because of its remarkably specific definition. We've all heard various well-intentioned sex experts declare that the size of the penis is not the most important thing, but we have yet to hear any of them say that they would like to trade places with a man who has a **micropenis.**

compare **brachyphallic, peniculas, subvirate**

misandrist /*MIZ and rist*/ n • A hater of men.

This is the counterpart to the well-known *misogynist* (hater of women). A **misandrist** is characterized by **misandry.**

"Lily made a sizable fortune running a dating school that taught wealthy and conversationally inept men how to behave in order to snare a partner. Unfortunately, the experience caused her to become a lifelong **misandrist,** and she wound up retiring to live in the woods with her three cats."

mome /*MOME*/ n • A nitpicking critic.

[Anglicized form of *Momus,* the Greek god of ridicule]

A new four-letter word is a pretty rare find; one with a stinging definition, rarer still. What a treat, then, to encounter **mome** for the first time.

"Having milked his crude dung sculptures for all the free publicity a drummed-up controversy could muster, Antoine, the hip and thoroughly untalented new artist, needed a new gimmick. But when people reacted with boredom to his vomit paintings, he lashed out cattily, saying, 'Everybody's a **mome.'** "

compare **zoilus**

monotonist /*mon OT un ist*/ n • A person who constantly speaks on only one subject.

It takes time to realize that the person one is talking to is a **monotonist.** Suspicion may arise after just a few minutes, but one does not know for sure until several hours have passed. By then it is too late; one has already squandered a small but precious portion of one's life on an intolerable bore.

"As his stultifying date with Sophie dragged into its third hour, Sam realized why this stunning woman did not have a boyfriend: She was a horrible **monotonist** whose conversation consisted entirely of endless prattle about her collection of pewter figurines."

mouchard /*moo SHARD*/ n • A spy in the employ of the police.

While **mouchard** will probably never replace "rat" in gangster lingo, one cannot deny that the word does have a certain panache.

"Throughout the East End, the name 'Steven Abramowitz' struck fear into the hearts of all the other criminals and riffraff. He was rumored to have once drowned a man in a urinal. What was not known, however, was that he was also a **mouchard** who would drop a dime on his own grandmother if it would keep the bobbies from shutting down his underground bingo empire."

mulierose /*MOO lee er ose*/ adj • Addicted to the love of women.

"Ivan had been **mulierose** for so long, he thought of it as a way of life. Then he met Cleo, the transvestite with a voice of silver and a heart of gold, and he enjoyed their fleeting romance so much that it prompted a midlife crisis he never fully worked through."

compare raddled

mumblecrust */MUM bl crust/* n • A toothless old beggar.

Some readers might think it rather cruel to refer to a toothless old beggar as a **mumblecrust**. The authors disagree. Attention, all you bleeding hearts out there! (In the unlikely event that any of you are still with us this far into the book.) We say that the word **mumblecrust** can be employed with sensitivity and understanding.

"Get out of my store, you foul **mumblecrust!**" shrieked the fishmonger's wife. She had caught the tattered hobo eyeing a pocket-sized perch, and was now chasing after him with a broom, raising clouds of dust and fleas in the process."

compare cadator

muscod */MUSS cod/* n • A perfumed fop; a man who wears too much scent.

Much as spices were originally sought out to mask the taste of spoiled meat, so was perfume developed to hide the stench of people's unwashed bodies. As we in civilized society have grown more conversant with the notion of personal hygiene, one would imagine that the need for perfume would diminish. But while some people have accepted this, there are plenty of others who seem to feel it is their primary duty in life to sail about assaulting the olfactory senses of their fellows.

"Vincent loved the smell of his aftershave, but was always somewhat disappointed when its sharp, tangy scent would begin to fade away twenty minutes or so after he put it on. Reasoning that if he couldn't smell it, it wasn't working, the **muscod** typically slathered on a quarter of a bottle at a time."
compare **odorivector, stinkard**

myrmidon /*MUR mid on*/ n ● A ruthless follower.
A word of classical origin: In Homer's *Iliad*, the **Myrmidons** were the brutal and fanatically obedient warrior followers of Achilles. According to myth, Zeus created them out of ants as subjects for Achilles' grandfather, King Aeacus. Aeacus beheld an anthill, and every ant became a **Myrmidon.**
compare **fanaticise, knipperdollin**

mysophiliac /*miz o FEEL ee ak*/ n ● A person who is sexually excited by filth or excretions.
"Ruth wished that she had listened to the admonitions of her hippie parents, who warned her that while it was fine to experiment, she would eventually grow out of her **mysophiliac** phase. Living in a yurt behind the abattoir with the town garbage-picker was beginning to lose some of its charm."
compare **eproctolagniac**

· N ·

naffin /*NAFF in*/ n   ●   One who is almost an idiot.

Some recipes call for garlic; for others, shallots will do. When the word *idiot* is a little too strong for the occasion, try **naffin** instead.

"Ever since the sad day poor old Fenton fell off the church steeple, the town fathers had been seeking a replacement for their beloved village idiot. Qualified applicants were hard to find, however, and the townsfolk had to suffer through a series of make-do **naffins** in the meantime."

compare **dunderwhelp, mattoid**

natiform /*NAT if orm*/ adj   ●   Shaped like the buttocks.

Off the top of one's head, it is difficult to think of something that cries out to be described as **natiform.** No matter; this word is obviously not complimentary, and opportunities to employ it will surely arise.

"The team of explorers felt a collective shiver run down their spines. Stretched before them was a sight never before

NAFFIN

seen by Western eyes: the mating grounds of the fabled and **natiform** Butter Pygmies."

compare **apoglutic, kakopygian, unipygic**

neoteny /*nee OT en ee*/ n ● The retention of juvenile characteristics into adulthood.

"When he awoke the morning after his fortieth birthday with a truly meaningful hangover, strapped to the remains of what had once been his waterbed, Wedgewood thought to himself, 'This **neoteny** must end.' "

compare **anaclitic**

nihilarian /*NAI ih LAIR ee an*/ n ● A person with a meaningless job.

"Having trouble dragging yourself to the office? Dpressed because your job is a pointless treadmill? Don't be glum! **Nihilarian** Career Services can help. We train thousands for exciting careers in such fields as iguana grooming, figurine arranging, and electric toothbrush repair. Send for our free brochure today!"

compare **aidle, fustilarian, ploiter**

novercant /*NO ver kant*/ adj ● Behaving like a stepmother.

"It was only her third date with their father, and already Ingrid was addressing the twins in severe, **novercant** tones, admonishing them not to wipe their mouths on their sleeves and the like. When the clumsy busboy spilled the hot tea on her lap, they could not contain their glee."

nullimitus */null IM it us/* n • A male virgin.

"Sick and tired of being the only **nullimitus** in his social circle, one evening Samuel got drunk enough to drive down to Tijuana to rectify the situation. Before he knew what was happening, he was on stage in a strip club, bound and gagged, while a mustachioed grandmother had her way with him."

compare **demivierge, subvirate**

· O ·

odorivector */O dor ih VEK tor/* n • The source of a smell.

Ah, the source of a smell. The fragrant rose; the pine woods in springtime; the loaf of fresh-baked bread. But let us leave these pleasant aromas behind for a moment, and turn instead to those offensive odors whose source is our fellow man.

Smell is invisible, and everyone is born immune to his own fetid emanations. That is why we often find ourselves looking an unwitting **odorivector** in the eye while straining not to breathe or audibly choke. It is a difficult posture to maintain, as the urge to flee or to douse the guilty party with a bucketful of mouthwash quickly builds.

"Although they tried to make the best of things, summertime just wasn't the same at the inner-city day camp after the budget cuts took hold. Instead of taking the kids swimming, counselors would march them to the public library to play 'find the **odorivector**.' "

compare **autosmia, diamerdis, muscod**

omnifutuant */om nee FOO tyoo ant/* adj ● Prone to engage in sexual activity with anything.

"Many readers were puzzled by the ad that ran in the Personals for several weeks that spring: 'Single Male **Omnifutuant,** seeking entity for romance on hot summer nights. Sex, age, species unimportant. Breathes oxygen a plus.' "

compare **animalist, anthropozoophilic,
avisodomy, hippomanic**

oniomaniac */o nee o MAY nee ak/* n ● A person with an unreasonable and uncontrollable impulse to buy things.

"Spending money was the only thing that Rupert's **oniomaniac** wife enjoyed doing, and even though the bills she ran up threatened to ruin him, he just didn't have the heart to take away her shopping privileges. He finally settled on buying the woman her own department store."

opisthotonicke */o PISS tho TON ik/* n ● A short-necked person.

"What a coup for Julie and her sorority sisters! Finally one of their mixers had attracted the biggest prize of all: a pod of beer-guzzling, butt-pinching **opisthotonickes** from the varsity football team. Her heart swelled with pride."

compare **brachyphallic**

· P ·

parepithymia */pa rep ith EYE mee uh/* n ● Perverted cravings due to mental illness.

"Faced with the prospect of losing his girlfriend's **parepithymia** due to her psychiatrist's meddling, Gavin took action and replaced her prescription medication with harmless little sugar pills."

compare **hogminny**

pathodixiac */path o DIX ee ak/* n ● One who pretends to be ill in order to garner sympathy.

There is almost nothing as irritating as this species of self-involved bore. **Pathodixiacs** abuse our sympathy, holding us hostage with their interminable tales of woe. No, we are not interested in your wheat allergy, thank you very much. If only muteness were one of your complaints, or deafness one of ours.

"After enduring months of listening to Lucille the **pathodixiac** complain about an illness they all knew to be

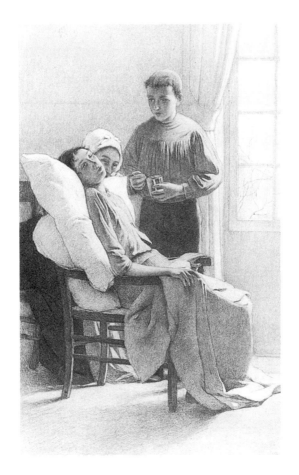

PATHODIXIAC

PECCABLE

imaginary, her coworkers decided to validate her and spiked her lunch with a hefty dose of salmonella."

compare **egrote**

peccable */PEK uh bul/* adj ● Liable to sin.

[Latin *peccare* to sin]

How strange that the word *impeccable* (meaning in its first sense "not capable of sinning"), which applies to no one, should survive the test of time while the seemingly much more useful **peccable** has fallen by the linguistic wayside.

peniculas /pen IK yoo las/ n • An undersized penis.

[Latin *peniculas* small penis]

The authors, being themselves male, feel an obligation to observe a certain code of honor and not make fun of other members of their gender for this most personal of shortcomings. That said, there is also an obligation to all readers to adequately present the most correct and specific form of opprobrium for each and every situation.

"Hampton had finally built up enough nerve to take out an ad in the Personals boldly stating that he was a SWM/**Peniculas,** but the letters of derision he received so outnumbered the inquisitive ones that he decided to give up dating forever."

compare **brachyphallic, micropenis, subvirate**

perissotomist /peh rih SOT o mist/ n • A knife-happy surgeon.

We've all heard the horror stories: Someone enters a clinic to have a small growth removed and exits minus a rather large limb. Chalk another one up for the **perissotomist.**

petulcity /pet OOL sit ee/ n • Offensive forwardness.

This is the word to apply to the behavior of that singularly irritating sort of person who intrudes on everyone at one time or another. The kind who fifteen minutes after meeting you at a staid dinner party is asking you the most intimate questions about your love life (and worse still, offering vivid descriptions

PETULCITY

of his own). Try jabbing him in the thumb webbing with a salad fork; if your hosts are at all gracious, they will understand.

compare **klazomaniac**

philodox */FAI lo dox/* n • A person in love with his own opinions.

Everybody has opinions. The **philodox,** however, is overly found of his or her own, and not fond enough of yours. The next time you encounter one of these insufferable people, it may cheer you slightly to know the proper word.

compare **sophomaniac**

philosophaster /fil OSS o fast er/ n • One who pretends to be knowledgeable about philosophy.

Philosophers have a long history of being hated by nearly everybody, including their own colleagues. Why, then, is the pejorative term **philosophaster** even necessary? Isn't "philosopher" a stinging enough insult in itself? One guess is that these miscreants came up with the term themselves to use in insulting one another.

compare **philodox**

pinchback /PINCH back/ n • Someone who is so miserly that he or she will not buy clothes.

"Fidel, incorrigible **pinchback** that he was, possessed but one pair of threadbare trousers, of indeterminate hue. When dining out, he would often pick up the check—then fling it down again and run into the men's room until someone else paid it."

compare **pinchgut**

pinchgut /PINCH gut/ n • Someone who is so miserly that he or she will not buy food.

"Growing up with a **pinchgut** for a father was a terrible chore. Whereas most families would order a pizza and eat it all at once, we had to eat the cheese and sauce off the top on the first day, and the following day we would get to eat the crust."

compare **pinchback, swedge**

pissburnt /PISS burnt/ adj • Stained with urine.

The thrifty reader is advised to remember the word **pissburnt** whenever he or she is tempted to drag home a "perfectly good, just slightly discolored" mattress that someone has put out on the sidewalk.

"Clayton was very much disgusted when the appraiser informed him that the centerpiece of his living room set, what he had believed to be an exquisite eighteenth-century damask settee, was actually a cheap loveseat, most likely manufactured in Eastern Europe, **pissburnt** and stained by the sun."

compare **bepiss, leint**

pleionosis /*PLAY o NO sis*/ n   ●   An exaggerated sense of one's own importance.

"After he lost his job to corporate downsizing, Dudley bought himself a cab. On his days off he would amuse himself by picking up only the most officious-looking businessmen at the airport and then intentionally getting stuck in traffic jams. It warmed the cockles of his heart to hear their squealing voices dripping with **pleionosis** in the back seat: 'You don't understand! I have a *very* important meeting to attend!' "

compare **autotheist, cockalorum**

ploiter /*PLOY ter*/ v   ●   To labor ineffectually.

A fine and memorable little word, suitable-sounding for its definition. **Ploiter** can be applied to amateurs and professionals alike, and to those who try hard at a given task as well as those whose hearts are just not in it.

"This year's convention of the United Gasket Changers' Union featured a full and varied agenda, headed by the keynote speech, "How Best to **Ploiter** for Your Union.""

compare **aidle, eyeservant**

plorabunde /*PLORE uh bund*/ n ● A person who weeps excessively.

"Her friends didn't understand how she could remain married to such a **plorabunde,** for Jasmine's husband would frequently spend half the night weeping quietly in bed. But she had long ago taught herself to cope by just lying there and pretending that she was asleep until it was over."

compare **begrutten, rectopathic**

plunderbund /*PLUN der bund*/ n ● A thieving group of businessmen.

There are several terms in the English language for a thieving group of businessmen, such as *Democrats, Republicans,* and *network executives.* **Plunderbund** can be used interchangeably with any of these.

compare **malversation**

plutomaniac /*PLOOT o MAY nee ak*/ n ● A person under the delusion that he or she is wealthy.

"Charlie Dawkins, **plutomaniac** and wino, would spend his entire welfare check on the first day, happily lying on a park bench and gorging on foie gras and Rhinish wine. The remainder of the month he subsisted on muscatel and canned sardines."

compare **callomaniac, sophomaniac**

poger /*POJ er*/ n ● A passive and older male homosexual.

"By day, it seemed a typical stodgy English public school. The crisp autumnal air resounded with the crack of cricket bats and with choruses of upper-class scions reciting Greek and Latin. But by night the school transformed itself into a pit of iniquity, with fresh-faced young students and hoary old professors alike engaging in lantern-lit bacchanals featuring unspeakable amusements, with the evening's proceedings often culminating in a frenzied ritual known as 'Roger the **Poger.**' "

compare **ingler, sodomitess**

pogogniasis /PO go NAI uh sis/ n ● Growth of a beard on a woman.

"As head of public relations for the international poultry conglomerate, one of Chelsea's least favorite duties was to deny any link between the hormones used in the vast chicken plants and the persistent outbreaks of **pogogniasis** afflicting the Central American villagers."

On rainy days I'll reminisce
the pretty girls I've got to kiss.
And try to forget
the few I regret;
*the ones with **pogogniasis**.*

compare **androgalactozemia, crurotrichosis**

porknell /PORK nell/ n ● A person who resembles a fat pig.

"The raft was small, the water supply was running low, and the last of the food had run out days ago. Jacob the **porknell** was beginning to feel distinctly uncomfortable with the hungry looks the other castaways were giving him."

compare **blowmaunger, pursy**

pricklouse */PRIK louse/* n ● A pejorative term for a tailor.

Oh, what a supple and colorful language English is! What other tongue could so elegantly and contemptuously conjure up the image of a poor slob sewing away on a flea-infested pair of trousers?

proxenetism */prok SEN it ism/* n ● Pimping performed by a female.

"Nobody in the small town where she grew up would have guessed that Dorothy's much-vaunted matchmaking abilities at the penny socials would eventually lead her to the far more lucrative world of **proxenetism** in the big city."

compare **dietairistriae**

psaphonic */saf ON ik/* adj ● Seeking fame and glory for oneself.

In ancient Libya there lived a man named Psapho, who was clever enough to realize that most people will listen to a talking animal before they listen to another person. So he taught an enormous host of parrots to say the words "Psapho is a god" (see **autotheist**) and then set them free, after which he was worshipped by many of the locals. Thus this word was born.

"Oscar figured that if he could get a rumor going among the female students concerning his lovemaking prowess, he would have his pick of the campus nubiles. So he hit upon the **psaphonic** plan of scrawling anonymous complimentary messages about his sexual expertise—and equipment—on bathroom walls throughout the college. Unhappily for him, he did not possess the nerve to invade the women's bathrooms for this purpose, and so he ended up being dogged by the wrong kind of rumors."

psychrotic /*sai KROT ik*/ adj ● Sexually frigid.

It is hard to say whether its similarity to *psychotic* helps this word or hurts it. Regardless, **psychrotic** is useful for alluding to what is an unfortunate condition.

compare **anorgasmic, dyspareunia**

pursy /*PURSE ee*/ adj ● Fat and short of breath.

"We on the hiking trip had grown weary of dragging the **pursy** Melissa along with us. Forever gobbling candy bars and begging for a rest, she was a nuisance to us all. On the third day we left her behind at daybreak, with half a canteen of water and two sticks of nougat."

compare **blowmaunger, porknell**

· Q ·

quaestuary /*KWESS tyoo air ee*/ n · One who is interested only in profit.

"Dennis, the real-estate **quaestuary**, simply could not understand why anyone would criticize his decision to raze the orphanage to make way for yet another golf course. 'Come *on*,' he would say with great incredulity. 'Do you have any idea how much *money* we're talking about here?' "

compare **barathrum, rabiator**

quibberdick /*KWIB er dik*/ n · A nasty quibbler.

The good thing about the word **quibberdick** is that people are not likely to mistake it for a compliment—even if they are not sure exactly what it means.

"Oh, how quickly the bloom came off the rose! Mona had only just begun to fall for the seemingly gallant Francesco when a petulant little incident over which movie to see revealed him to be a shrill and small-minded **quibberdick.** Now he stood about as much chance of sharing her bed as a diseased porcupine."

compare **baratress, breedbate**

· R ·

rabiator */RAY bee ate or/* n ● A violent and greedy person.

"Of course it was just the luck of the draw, but the Sawyers couldn't help but feel a bit cheated. It didn't seem fair that some lucky family abroad was getting their angel of a son for nine months, while in exchange they had to provide room and board to an ill-tempered **rabiator** who threw terrible tantrums whenever his meals were less than huge, and who always had poppy seeds stuck between his orange teeth."

compare **barathrum**

rabulistic */rab yoo LIST ik/* adj ● Characterized by legal trickery.

"It was a huge success on the mystery theater circuit, although everyone seemed to take *The **Rabulistic** Murders* for a feel-good comedy, perhaps because of the scene in which the drunken mob beat the three lawyers to death with their own briefcases."

compare **barrator, leguleian**

raddled /RAD uld/ adj ● Aged and made worse by debauchery.

"The women at the ski lodge always looked forward to the yearly arrival of Sven, he of the drunken nocturnal romps in the snow. Alas, this year the aging lothario had grown so thoroughly **raddled** that the best he could come up with was a desultory pinch on the buttocks for most of them."

compare **blowze, mulierose**

ranivorous /ran IV or us/ adj ● Frog-eating.

Like *delicate, showy, and skittish*, **ranivorous** is one of those rare adjectives that one can apply to both storks and Frenchmen.

compare **cepivorous, frenchified**

recrudescence /re crud ESS ence/ n ● The reappearance of a wound or sore; figuratively, the reappearance of something bad.

While the authors by no means wish to deprive the reader of the right to use the word **recrudescence** to describe those nasty sores that just won't go away, it is to be hoped that the word will play more of a figurative role in most vocabularies.

While romancing a winsome young doll,
my ex-wife just happened to call.
*This **recrudescence***
did cause my tumescence
to shrivel to nothing at all.

RECTOPATHIC

rectopathic /rek toe PATH ik/ adj ● Easily hurt emotionally.

Rectopathic people are always fun to tease. Unless you are completely devoid of talent in this area, it should be possible to drive one to tears in under fifteen minutes.

"Exasperated from constantly walking on eggshells in the office, Jameson decided to hurt the feelings of his **rectopathic** executive assistant one last time, sacking him over the Christmas holidays."

compare **anaclitic, begrutten, plorabunde**

ripesuck /RIPE suk/ n ● One who is easily bribed.

A fittingly revolting term for this concept.

"While all the other lobbyists worked the phones furiously, J. B. sipped his highball, unworried about the upcoming vote. Good thing his long experience in Washington had taught him how to spot a **ripesuck** at sixty yards."

compare **boodler, cacique**

ructuosity /ruk choo OSS it ee/ n ● Frequent belching.

"It started with a bunch of brewery workers belching in unison to make the time pass quickly on the assembly line. Now they sold out such venues as Carnegie Hall. But the Milwaukee **Ructuosity** Choir never let their success go to their heads."

rudesby /ROODS bee/ n ● A loud boor; a generally offensive person.

The **rudesby** is not on many people's endangered species

RIPESUCK

list. In fact, it often seems that this offensive creature is more common today than at any other time in history.

It has certainly never been more *fashionable* to be a **rudesby.** Hallmarks of this pest include a liking for brutish and vulgar forms of entertainment; vapid and profane speech; vicious pets; monstrous vehicles; and clownish attire.

In any case, **rudesby** is a memorable and useful word, and most people will understand what it means at once, even if they are hearing it for the first time.

"Brett did not consider himself to be a **rudesby.** Blasting rap music from his SUV's outward-facing speakers late at night in residential districts was for him a sacred form of self-expression."

• S •

scaff /SKAFF/ v • To beg for food in a contemptible fashion.

The authors' last book, *Depraved English*, included the word *groak*, meaning "to stare silently at someone while they are eating, in the hope that they will offer some food." **Scaffing** takes things a step further. At least the *groaker* maintains a semi-dignified posture while *groaking*; not so the **scaffer.**

"It was always the same thing with the little animals, whenever Ahmed brought food home. The whining, the drooling, the pawing at his clothes—all making it impossible for him to eat in peace. When was his brood of small children ever going to stop **scaffing** and learn to forage on their own?"

compare **lickspigot**

scaurous /SKOW russ/ adj • Having thick ankles.

"How all the girls hated the winsome Belinda. She was the prettiest girl at school, and all the boys longingly followed her with their eyes in the hallways between classes. When in the locker room one day the discovery was made that she was extraordinarily **scaurous**—and insecure about it—they leapt on this vulnerability like jackals on a stillborn antelope."

scombroid /*SKOM broid*/ adj ● Resembling a mackerel.

One of the odder words in the singularly descriptive and comprehensive language we call English. Few people have used it; fewer still to describe something without gills. Still, the reader is urged to commit it to memory. For who knows? One day the occasion may very well arise to insult a sallow, saucer-eyed, chinless, thick-lipped runt of a fellow. In this case, no other term will do.

scrag /*SKRAG*/ n ● A lean and bony person.

There is a glut of words for fat people in the English language. Terms for their skinny counterparts are sorely needed in order to provide some semblance of balance, especially today, with images of pouting, glamorized **scrags** festooning every billboard and magazine cover within eyeshot. Unfairly, such words are relatively few and far between, so make the most of **scrag.**

" 'You can never be too rich or too thin,' the unhappy little **scrag** said to herself, washing down her guilty feast of half a rice cake and a stalk of celery with a diet protein drink on her way home from aerobics class."

compare **chichiface, gammerstang**

screable /*SKREE uh bl*/ adj ● Which may be spit upon.

Every so often a city or municipality will wage some sort of public campaign exhorting its citizens to not spit so much, or

SCRAG

to not spit on the sidewalk. While these efforts are laudable, they really don't go far enough. Certainly sidewalks should not be the recipient of all this expectoration, at least not when there are so many **screable** people to go around. Indeed, life abounds with people who deserve to be spit on. So the next time you hawk and clear a gob of phlegm from your throat, hold on to it for a while; chances are it will not be long before your eye settles upon some eminently **screable** individual.

compare **bespawled, sialismus**

screeve /*SKREEV*/ n ● A begging letter.
v ● To write begging letters.

A writer of begging letters is known as a **screever.**

"Soaring tuition and a renewed emphasis on practical education led the small progressive college to require all incoming freshmen to take **Screeving** 101 in addition to algebra and a foreign language. Instead of a term paper, students had to convince their parents to wire them one thousand dollars to cover a fictional medical emergency."

compare **cadator, mumblecrust**

scybalous /*SIB il us*/ adj ● Resembling small, hardened chunks of feces that can form in a diseased colon (*scybala*).

Sure, this is an obscure medical term that nobody will understand should you whip it out in an argument, but who cares? Off the top of one's head, one would be hard-pressed to think of a more offensive thing to say to someone than that they resemble a small and hardened fecal mass lodged inside a diseased internal organ.

compare **coproma**

seeksorrow /SEEK *sorrow*/ n ● One who seeks to give himself vexation.

This word applies to everybody at one time or another. For reasons that are hard to understand, we do such things as venture to the mall the day after Thanksgiving, try to fix our own plumbing, and become fans of losing sports teams (as well as fall in love, have babies, and go on family vacations).

shilpit /SHILL *pit*/ adj ● 1) Feeble, puny, or sickly. 2) Weak, good-for-nothing, or watered-down.

With its various definitions, all clustering around the notion of worthless, **shilpit** is a good meat-and-potatoes type of general insult. Happily for us all, it can be used to describe just about anything. . . .

*There was once a **shilpit** man*
*living in a **shilpit** house.*
*He drove a **shilpit** car*
*and wed a **shilpit** spouse.*

*He had a **shilpit** job*
to which he had to go.
*And sipped a **shilpit** beer*
*watching a **shilpit** show.*

compare **imbonity**

shotclog /SHOT *klog*/ n ● An unpleasant drinking companion, tolerated only because he or she is buying the drinks.

(This particular form of generosity will absolve many sins.)

"As a **shotclog** par excellence, Woodrow was able to transform his inheritance into a form of social acceptance, at least among the circle of alcoholic artists who despised him, yet whose company he preferred."

compare spunger

sialismus */sai uh LIZ muss/* n • An excessive flow of saliva.

The problem with people afflicted with **sialismus** is not just that they have too much spit in their mouths. It is the fact that they often seem to be hell-bent on sharing it with the world when they talk. Nobody loves a spitter. Not even his own mother.

"As a rock-star wannabe with a death wish, Henderson secretly felt that choking on his own vomit—as so many of his musical idols had done before him—would be 'a good way to go out.' He almost, but not quite, got his wish when his **sialismus** caused him to drown painlessly in his own spittle while sleeping one night."

compare bespawled, screable

skimmington */SKIM ing ton/* n • A ceremony in which a man whose wife beat him or cheated on him was publicly ridiculed.

The **skimmington** had its heyday in English villages several hundred years ago. However one feels about the social climate of that time and place, one must admit those English villagers possessed a real sense of community.

"It was ratings month again, and just like clockwork all the daytime talk shows put their best foot forward: nothing but big breasts and surprise **skimmingtons** would grace the airwaves for the next four weeks."

compare legruita, wetewold

slockster /SLOK ster/ n ● One who entices away another's servants.

Slockster is one of those words that provide a notion of how people lived in the past. Because formerly the issue of stealing away servants must have been an important one, or there would have been no need for such a word. Then, as now, good help was probably hard to find. Today most people don't have servants, but a kind of **slockster** is common enough in other areas of the labor market, such as professional sports.

"Judge Hobarth had made a lot of enemies upholding the law. When the time came for his reelection, vicious rumors of mysterious origin began to circulate—how he was an atheist, a drunk, and a **slockster.**"

slotterhodge /SLOT er hoj/ n ● A messy eater.

"It was always an ordeal dining with Mr. and Mrs. **Slotterhodge,** and their gross corpulence only made their contemptible manners less excusable. Dribbling gravy from their chins, leaning over one's plate with their mouths full, and asking hopefully, 'You using that drumstick?' they made me want to vomit."

compare **gundygut**

smeke /SMEEK/ v ● To go too far in one's flattery.

"Ingratiating small talk was Casey's specialty. But as soon as the words were out of his mouth, he realized he had **smeked** badly by referring in passing to his host's 'beautiful daughter.' In reality, the girl in question strongly resembled a monkey on the Nature Channel. The

SLOTTERHODGE

question was, could he backtrack without making things worse?"

compare **fart-sucker, subsycophant**

sneckdraw */SNEK draw/* n • One who stealthily enters a house; a thief. Hence, any sly, crafty person.

"All the campers were supposed to go to the lake for swimming lessons, but Ferdinand, the eight-year-old **sneck-draw,** had other ideas. Backtracking to the cabins on tiptoe, he made directly for the bunks of those children who had received care packages, and spent the next hour gorging on all manner of candy. He then he wet his hair, grabbed his towel, and hid along the path to fall in step with the returning troop."

compare **snudge**

snivelard /SNIV uh lard/ n • Someone who speaks through the nose; a whiny person.

With its similarity to *sniveler*, **snivelard** certainly has a contemptible cast to it. It is another example (see **clatterfart**) of a very insulting-looking word that has an only slightly insulting definition. Such words are useful when one wishes to heap scorn upon someone but lacks better ammunition. Some pretty good insults can be formed thusly, as in "I am not in the habit of arguing with **snivelards.** And you, sir, are a **snivelard.**"

"The smarmy and repugnant little **snivelard** at the Help Desk so offended Marcie that when he turned his back for a moment she struck him in his bald spot with the courtesy phone, then acted like nothing had happened as he whined through his nose in pain."

snollygoster /SNOLL ee GOSS ter/ n • An unprincipled person, especially a politician.

"Ethan knew that his opponent didn't really have sex with pigs, but he also knew that it would steal momentum from his campaign if he had to take time out to deny the rumor. And before anyone could squeal foul, the young **snollygoster** had won his third consecutive term as president of the high school debating society."

compare **boodler, empleomaniac, malversation, ripesuck**

snool /*SNOOL*/ v ● To depress someone by constantly chiding or nagging him or her.

"Three days into the vacation with his wife, two children, and sister-in-law, Artie was so thoroughly **snooled** that he could do little more than hunker in the back of the camper, sobbing quietly into his can of Dinty Moore."

SNOOL

132

snoutband /SNOUT band/ n ● One who constantly interrupts his or her companions in order to contradict them.

"Goddard tried ignoring him, spilling his drink on him, even farting in his general direction. Nothing, however, but nothing would deter the cursed little **snoutband** seated to his right at the dinner party, the one torpedoing every one of his attempts to make a good impression with the ladies by contradicting all of his carefully constructed lies."

snudge /SNUℑ/ n ● A scoundrel who hides under the bed, waiting for a chance to rob the house.

"Patience was the key to Wolfgang's status as a world-class **snudge**. Of course, it also helped to have a slender physique and a bladder several times normal size."

compare **sneckdraw**

sodomitess /sod o mit ESS/ n ● A female sodomite, in the passive sense.

A thievish stockbroker named Mel
was housed with an inmate from Hell.
*No **sodomitess***
e'er felt such distress
as he felt every night in his cell.

compare **ingler, poger**

sophomaniac /soff o MAY nee ak/ n ● One under the delusion that he or she is wise.

Sophomania is a common and deeply irritating condition

133

that can crop up in any type of person. It is especially rife, however, among those with a little too much education. A word to the (genuinely) wise: Don't waste your time arguing with **sophomaniacs.** It is far better to ignore them completely, or poke them in the eye.

compare **callomaniac, philosophaster, plutomaniac**

sporge /SPORJ/ v ● To be afflicted with diarrhea.

Seen on the page, the word **sporge** looks like it could mean just about anything, from the sound of a bouncing rubber ball to one of the ingredients in a mesclun salad. What a pleasant surprise to find that it actually means to be afflicted with the runs.

INSTRUCTIVE RHYME FOUND SCRAWLED INSIDE A PORT-O-POTTY AT THE ANNUAL GASTRO-ENDOCRINOLOGISTS' CLAMBAKE:

If on shellfish we gorge,
*Then soon we will **sporge.***

compare **imbulbitate, sterky**

spuddle /SPUD l/ v ● To attend to trifling matters as though they were of the greatest importance.

As a derisive term to describe the overofficious behavior of self-important people, **spuddle** is invaluable. In fact, anyone who has ever held a job should be familiar with the **spuddler.** Career advancement is often bestowed upon those employees who can **spuddle** more convincingly than their coworkers.

"No one had the heart to mock Haverford, the consumptive little office boy, for adopting a ludicrous aura of solemnity every time he doled out the new vials of correction fluid to the staff. Apparently, **spuddling** afforded the poor sod his main satisfaction in life."

compare beadledom

spunger /SPUN jer/ n ● One who drinks at the expense of another.

This is the flip side of a **shotclog**. We have all known **spungers**. Many of us have even aspired to be one.

Especially as they are pronounced the same, the reader might well ask what is the real difference between a **spunger** with a "u" and the familiar *sponger* with an "o." Well, this particular spelling also seems to go along with a more specific definition, at least according to Thomas Wright's *Dictionary of Obsolete and Provincial English* of 1857.

"Who came out ahead? It was hard to say. The friendless and socially inept tavern owner footed the bill for round after round of whiskeys, but the pathetic **spungers** gathered around him at the end of the bar had to pretend to enjoy his company, and to be interested in his endless stories that went nowhere. It was a sad situation all around."

compare shotclog

sterky /STIR kee/ adj ● Loose in the bowels from fear.

Some people have a tendency to get **sterky** in sticky situations. Perhaps it is a vestige from some primeval defense mechanism—befouling oneself as a last resort to avoid the jaws of the lion.

" 'Are you *sure* everything's all right in there, sir?' F. W.'s executive assistant asked worriedly, knocking again on the bolted bathroom door. The stockholders in the crowded meeting hall were getting restless while their **sterky** CEO cowered on the toilet, terrified of having to answer publicly for the bad quarterly report."

Said the doelike young man from Turkey,
whose walk was alarmingly jerky,
"It's not that I'm lame
enfeebled or game,
*it's just that I'm constantly **sterky**."*

compare **ankyloproctia, imbulbitate**

stinkard /STINK ard/ n • One who stinks.

A very special word for a very special person: he who stinks. Some **stinkards** are unaware of their stench, of course. Others just don't care.

"Finding work for Marcus, a confirmed **stinkard** who had prioritized his right not to bathe, was proving to be a bit of a challenge for the folks at the employment agency. Having no openings for lighthouse-keepers, they finally got him a job as night watchman at the town dump."

compare **ablutophobic, diamerdis, muscod, odorivector**

strene /STREEN/ v • To copulate; said of a dog.

With its uncomfortable similarity to *strain*, **strene** is not much more genteel-sounding than the phrase *doggy-style*. But it does have benefit of being obtuse.

"Mr. and Mrs. Bullinger thought they had finally found a young couple willing to buy their split-level ranch, which they had been trying to sell for years. Things got off on the wrong foot the day of the house tour, however, when the neighbor's bulldog happened to be **strening** with a verminous mongrel in the front yard just as the prospective buyers arrived."

compare **amplexus, fream**

subsycophant /*sub SIK o fant*/ n ● A revolting parasite.

"The angels couldn't decide in what form to reincarnate Sasha, for in life he had been such a revolting **subsycophant** that sending him back as a worm was too good for him. Finally, they elected to have him spend his next life as a blow-up sex doll, with the words 'up to 350 lbs. pressure' stamped on his left ankle."

compare **bdelloid, fart-sucker, lickspigot**

subvirate /*SUB vih rate*/ n ● One whose manhood is imperfect or undeveloped.

Subvirate is one of those delightfully descriptive words that are always handy to have around.

"Ettiene saw no reason why women, with their push-up bras and the like, should be the only ones to feel better about themselves by way of wearing an uncomfortable contraption. And so he fashioned a codpiece of sorts out of latex and foam, and marketed it to **subvirates** with a taste for tight clothing."

compare **badling, nullimitus, peniculas**

surd /*SURD*/ n ● A foolish and insensitive person.

[Latin *surdus* silent, mute, dumb]

"Finding that his new schoolmates already had a class bully and a class clown, Donahue took the bold step of combining the two roles, and as the class **surd** he would stomp about making farting noises while he tormented the smaller children."

swartwouter /*SWART wow ter*/ n ● A fleeing embezzler.
　"Police searched the city in vain for Manfredy, the wily **swartwouter,** but he was already halfway across the Atlantic with a tote bag full of junk bonds, chuckling softly to himself over his second Mai Tai."

compare **boodler**

swedge /*SWEJ*/ v ● To leave without paying one's bill.
Quoth the sallow young man from New York
as he gorged on milkshakes and pork,
*"I find when I **swedge***
that it gives me an edge
if I first stab the host with a fork."

compare **thrimmel**

symphoric /*sim FORE ik*/ adj ● Accident prone.
　"They had the patience of a dozen Jobs, the Butlers did, but eventually they grew tired of having to constantly safe-guard their house after their **symphoric** son hit his teen years. With dreams of childless vacations and savings on col-lege bills dancing through their heads, they began leaving metal forks near electrical outlets and investing in furniture with pointy edges."

compare **looby**

synechthry /*SIN ek three*/ n ● The state of living together in enmity.

———

Yes, it has a daunting spelling, and frankly the authors are not absolutely sure how to pronounce it. But simply knowing that there is a word out there that encapsulates this all-too-common situation is worth something, isn't it?

"Insisting that they were staying together 'for the children's sake,' the Dorchesters spent twenty-five years gritting their teeth at each other in **synechthry** and raised a fine brood, all of whom eventually graduated to loveless marriages of their own."

• T •

tartuffe */tar TOOF/* n • A religious hypocrite; one who affects piety.

[From the title character of a play by Molière]

A word like **tartuffe** presents a pleasing dilemma: namely, with such a wealth of potential targets at one's disposal, to whom does one apply the term? To the televangelist who rants against homosexuality while indulging in a wide variety of sexual pecadilloes? To the married congressman who professes a great love of the Scriptures, and meanwhile boinks a series of twenty-something aides? Yes! **Tartuffe** is an equal-opportunity word and should be employed liberally to describe all manner of religious hypocrites.

"Life at Sunday school had not been pleasant for young Linus; Father William in particular seemed to have it in for the young scamp. Then came that glorious day when he caught the wizened old **tartuffe** in a compromising position while frolicking in the holy water. In exchange for his silence,

TARTUFFE

Linus got to drink as much of the sacred wine as he wanted and sleep in the back pews during mass."

compare antinomian, eisegetical

testiculous /*tess TIK yoo luss*/ adj ● Having exceedingly large testicles.

[Latin *testiculus* testicle]

Certainly this word can be employed as a compliment, but it also has other uses. For instance, who hasn't at one time or another been treated to the grotesque but strangely riveting spectacle of some prim matron walking an enormous, **testiculous** dog down the street?

"No sultan of Siam ever sired more offspring than Gilbert, the **testiculous** milkman, whose forty-nine-year career spanned the man shortages of two world wars."

compare macromaniac

thrimmel /*THRIM el*/ v ● To pay a debt in a mean and niggardly fashion.

Here it is: the perfect word for those people who just can't pay up gracefully. All the world hates a **thrimmeller.** And yet this species of tightfist prospers.

"As a mob enforcer with intellectual aspirations, Luther enjoyed peppering his shakedowns with five-dollar words. 'Listen, bub,' he would say while hanging a debtor out the window by his ankles, 'Quit yer **thrimmelling,** or yer sidewalk pizza, see?'"

compare swedge

timeserver /*TIME serv er*/ n ● A person who changes his opinions to fit the times, or to be compliant with a superior.

These spineless jellyfish are everywhere. Their only talent, a pernicious knack for self-preservation, is enough to ensure that they will never be eradicated completely.

"As a high-level bureaucrat and professional **timeserver,** Beisswenger had so attuned his sensitive antennae to the slightest shift in the political winds that he had managed to survive five different administrations. As for his official duties, no one could remember what they were."

compare **ecomaniac, fart-sucker**

tittery-whoppet /*TIT er ee WOP it*/ n ● An archaic euphemism for the vagina.

Although this word is not exactly an insult, it is the most absurd euphemism for the female genitalia that the authors have found after many months of diligent searching. It is difficult to imagine how one could retain even a spark of ardor after saying or hearing this word during a romantic encounter. "Oh! Darling! That's it . . . touch my **tittery-whoppet!**"

On the flip side of the coin, the silliest term for the penis that the authors have yet seen is probably *Polyphemus*. Polyphemus was the original one-eyed monster, the cyclops that devoured several of Ulysses' men. Aside from being somewhat obtuse, this word is also quaintly hopeful. Doubtless there is an allusion from the classics denoting a crippled, half-blind midget that would be far more fitting than that of a mighty, towering, single-eyed monster, but we don't know what it is.

compare **aerocolpos, licktwat**

tosspot /*TOSS pot*/ n • A drunkard.

[From the phrase *to toss a pot*, to drink a pot]

What a charming and evocative little word **tosspot** is. Should it be updated to take into account the alcohol receptacles of today? *Tossbottle* has a nice ring to it.

"Hank, the neighborhood **tosspot,** could never seem to get his old pickup truck off blocks and running again. But he just loved to tinker, and much to the consternation of his neighbors he spent the better part of every weekend whaling away under the hood with a ball-peen hammer while abominably drunk."

compare **barlichood, debacchate**

TOSSPOT

trugabelly /*TRUG uh bell ee*/ n ● A short and dirty fellow assigned to the most menial tasks.

This poor drudge is perhaps more an object of pity than scorn. On the other hand, who would not object to being called a **trugabelly?** Clearly this is not a *nice* word.

"Frustrated by her billionaire husband's lack of attention, the trophy wife had no recourse but to lavish all of her considerable affections upon the old **trugabelly** who manured the grounds on Tuesdays—the one with the gap-toothed smile."

compare **barkled**

tumbrel /*TUM brel*/ n ● 1) A cart that is used for transporting dung. 2) A person who is drunk to the point of vomiting.

While it can't hurt to know another way to refer to a dung cart, the second definition of this word is more germane. The next time an overly soused guest deposits his dinner on your bathroom floor, you will be able to refrain from issuing a hackneyed batch of expletives and instead correctly peg him with the proper terminology.

turdefy /*TURD if eye*/ v ● To turn into feces.

[*turd* from Old English *tord* + *-fy* to make]

A point of usage: It is the authors' understanding that this verb can be both transitive and intransitive. That is, it can refer to the act of becoming shit as well as the act of turning something else into shit.

"After his new sous-chef **turdified** the rack of lamb—in addition to the black bean soup, the *crème brulée*, and even the *frisée* greens—Chef Claude snapped his fingers and two burly dishwashers whisked the unlucky lad into the walk-in freezer. The wily old veteran of the backbiting culinary wars was not born yesterday; interrogation quickly determined which of his competitors had sent the saboteur."

compare alothen

twee */TWEE/* adj • Overly cute.

"Jessie tried very hard to get along with his dorm mate, a twee surfer boy who always wore pastels and was rather *too* fond of unicorns. Alas, it proved to be impossible, and the two of them spent the rest of the semester maintaining a sullen silence."

twitchel */TWICH ul/* n • A childish old man.

"Ever since his stroke last August, Mr. Dodwell had become more and more of a twitchel. What a tragedy it was to see the once-proud drill sergeant reduced to a squalling brat who would cry when he didn't get a sweetie after dinner."

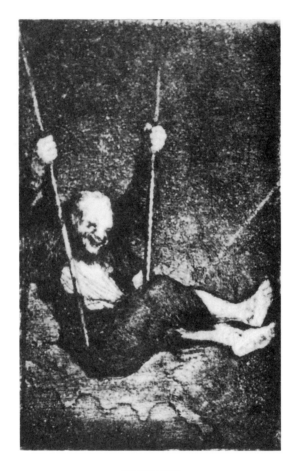

TWITCHEL

ᐧ U ᐧ

ucalegon */yoo KAL eh gon/* n ● A neighbor whose house is on fire.

[From the name of a Trojan chieftan whose house was set ablaze by the Greeks]

Not a word to use every day, and not a particularly insulting one, either. But the authors still feel that **ucalegon** is interesting enough to warrant inclusion in the present volume. If life ever does offer an opportunity to use this word, you would be wise to seize it, as another chance may never come.

"Mingling with the crowd gathered outside the burning dwelling, the ill-starred lexicographer simply could not restrain himself; after smugly flaunting the word **ucalegon** several dozen times, he was set upon by his neighbors and cast into the flames."

compare **epicaricacy**

unasinous */yoo NASS in us/* adj ● Equally stupid.

[Latin *unus* one + *asinus* ass]

The reader may well wonder how to employ such a word,

148

but **unasinous** is more useful than it first appears. For instance, in describing both sides of a foolish argument.

"Controlled experiments with the Chinese finger trap proved what the townsfolk had suspected all along: the Underhill twins were indeed **unasinous.**"

unipygic */yoo ni PIE gik/* adj ● Having but one ass cheek.

[Latin *unus* one + Greek *pyge* rump]

Literally, half-assed.

A good word for veiled insults:

". . . And so I introduce to you, ladies and gentlemen, the man whose **unipygic** leadership has brought this company to where it is today. . . ."

compare **apoglutic, kakopygian**

uriposiac */yoo rip O zee ak/* n ● A drinker of urine.

[Greek *ouron* urine + *posis* drinking]

Yes, they do shoot horses, and some people do drink urine. Why? In certain circles it is held to be medically beneficial to drink your first batch of the day (Gandhi is reported to have quaffed a cup of his own special home brew every morning). Other folks like to imbibe someone else's; maybe they just like the taste.

"The ideological battle at the clinic was fast becoming an ugly one. Now the **uriposiac** camp of doctors attempted to take the upper hand by secretly spiking the patient's IV bags with their panacea. The results were not encouraging."

compare **leint**

uzzard */UZZ ard/* n • A third-generation bastard.

"Many were the nights that Stevens the **uzzard,** after consuming too much crème de menthe, would rise to his feet and loudly proclaim his pride in his heritage, or lack thereof. 'My father was a bastard,' he would declare slurringly, 'and his father before him was a bastard as well!' "

compare **adulterine, yaldson**

· V–Z ·

ventose /*ven TOSE*/ adj • Verbally flatulent; full of pomp, conceit, and bombast.

[Latin *ventus* wind]

"Because of the **ventose** talk show host's ability to fill endless hours of airtime with his inane rantings, the very same quality that had always caused most people to loathe him instantly was now making him a very rich man indeed."

compare **blatherskite, cacafuego**

verbigerator /*ver BIG er ATE or*/ n • One who senselessly repeats clichés.

"People considered him an old sage, and his advice was eagerly sought by luminaries from far and wide. No one seemed to realize that Hanson was nothing more than a senile old **verbigerator** with a talent for continually firing off platitudes."

compare **echolalia**

vetanda /ve TAN duh/ n,pl ● Things that should not be done.

There are so many things in life that should not be done, and so many people doing them. It seems odd that the word for this concept is not more widely known.

The parson thought he might enjoy
a harmless tryst with Ms. Lacroix.
But the memoranda
*of their **vetanda***
was a club-footed, half-wit boy.

wetewold /WAIT wald/ n ● A patient cuckold.

[Middle English *cokewold* cuckold, with substitution of *wete* wit, to know]

"Tyson the **wetewold** knew that his wife was making time with most of his buddies, but he didn't care. As long as her extracurricular activities freed him up to play with his beloved electric trains, he was content."

compare **skimmington**

windbroach /WIND broach/ n ● An inferior fiddler.

Life is long, and one never knows when a necessity might arise to insult a lousy violinist—perhaps at the next fourth-grade talent show you attend. Be prepared: keep **windbroach** at the ready.

compare **cantabank**

woodpusher /WOOD push er/ n ● A poor chess player.

"Determined that their son would be the next Kasparov,

the Sigorskis refused to recognize that he was a **woodpusher** with more interest in dolls than in a chess board. Their insistence that he play the game sent him to the sanitarium before he was eleven."

yaldson /YALD son/ n • The son of a prostitute.

"Preston's upbringing in the bordello had been a happy one. He was lavished with attention from the girls, who lovingly called him 'Peaches' and would often braid flowers in his hair. It wasn't until his first day at the academy, when he heard the word **yaldson** uttered with scorn, that he felt a twinge of shame."

compare uzzard

yeevil /YEE vil/ n • A dung fork.

"The Richardsons set a most impressive table: china aplenty, serving plates and soup bowls abounding, and every conceivable type of utensil for each one of the innumerable courses they typically served during a formal meal. Given the miserable quality of the food itself, however, they might as well have given each guest a **yeevil** and left it at that."

zoilus /ZOY lus/ n • An envious person.

[From *Zoilus*, the name of a Greek famed for his criticisms of Homer]

"Andrew was cursed with a jealous and scheming faculty advisor. As he prepared his Ph.D. thesis, the man ridiculed and belittled him so mercilessly that he ended up abandoning his efforts to take a job teaching remedial education in a small rural high school. Several months later, the **zoilus** published the work under his own name."

compare **mome**

zowerswopped /*ZOW er swopt*/ adj • Foul-tempered.

If we've given cause to offend,
rest assured we'd never intend
to make you feel bad,
unpleasant, or sad,
with this zowerswopped book that we've penned.

A SELECT BIBLIOGRAPHY

The American Heritage Dictionary of the English Language. Boston: Houghton Mifflin Company, 1980.

The American Illustrated Medical Dictionary. 9th ed. Philadelphia and London: W. B. Saunders Company, 1918.

Bailey, Nathaniel. *An Universal Etymological English Dictionary*. 18th ed. London, 1761.

Black, Donald Chain. *Spoonerisms, Sycophants, and Sops*. New York: Harper and Row, 1988.

Black's Law Dictionary. 35th ed. Totowa, N.J.: Barnes and Noble Books, 1987.

Blake, Roger. *The American Dictionary of Sexual Terms*. Hollywood, Calif.: Century Publishing Co., 1964.

Bowler, Peter. *The Superior Person's Book of Words*. New York: Dell Laurel, 1982.

———. *The Superior Person's Second Book of Weird and Wondrous Words*. Boston: David R. Godine, 1992.

Brent, Irwin M., and Rod L. Evans. *More Weird Words*. New York: Berkley Books, 1995.

Byrne, Josefa Heifitz. *Mrs. Byrne's Dictionary of Unusual, Obscure and Preposterous Words*. New York: Citadel Press and University Books, 1974.

The Century Dictionary and Cyclopedia. New York: Century Company, 1889–1914.

Chambers, Ephraim. *Cyclopedia: Or, An Universal Dictionary of Arts and Sciences*. London: 1791.

Cockeram, Henry. *The English Dictionarie of 1623*. New York: Huntington Press, 1930.

The Compact Oxford English Dictionary. 2d ed. Oxford: Oxford University Press, 1991.

Davies, T. Lewis. *A Supplementary Glossary*. London: George Bell and Sons, 1881.

Dickson, Paul. *Words*. New York: Delacorte Press, 1982.

Dictionary of Psychology. 3d British Commonwealth ed. London: Peter Owen, 1972.

Dunglison, Robley. *A Dictionary of Medical Science*. Philadelphia: Henry C. Lea, 1874.

Dunkling, Leslie. *The Guiness Book of Curious Words*. Enfield, Middlesex: Guiness Publishing Ltd., 1994.

Ehrlich, Eugene. *The Highly Selective Dictionary for the Extraordinarily Literate*. New York: HarperCollins Publishers, 1997.

———. *The Highly Selective Thesaurus for the Extraordinary Literate*. New York: HarperCollins Publishers, 1994.

Elster, Charles Harrington. *There's a Word for It! A Grandiloquent Guide to Life*. New York: Pocket Books, 1996.

Funk and Wagnall's New Standard Dictionary of the English Language. Medallion Edition. New York: Funk and Wagnall's Company, 1942.

Goldenson, Robert, and Kenneth Anderson. *The Wordsworth Dictionary of Sex*. Hertfordshire: Wordsworth Editions Ltd., 1994.

Gordon, Dale. *The Dominion Sex Dictionary*. 1967.

Gould, George M. *An Illustrated Dictionary of Medicine, Biology, and Allied Sciences*. 4th ed. Philadelphia: P. Blakiston, Son & Co., 1898.

Grambs, David. *Dimboxes, Epopts, and Other Quidams*. New York: Workman Publishing, 1986.

———. *The Endangered English Dictionary*. New York: W. W. Norton & Company, 1994.

Grose, Francis. *1811 Dictionary of the Vulgar Tongue*. London: Bibliophile Books, 1984.

———. *A Provincial Glossary; With a Collection of Local Proverbs, and Popular Superstitions*. 2d ed. London: S. Hooper, 1790.

Halliwell, James Orchard. *Dictionary of Archaic Words*. London: Bracken Books, 1986.

Hellweg, Paul. *The Insomniac's Dictionary*. New York: Ballantine Books, 1986.

Hinsie, Leland E., and Robert Campbell. *Psychiatric Dictionary*. New York: Oxford University Press, 1960.

Hook, J. N. *The Grand Panjandrum*. New York: Macmillan Publishing Company, 1980.

Hughes, Geoffrey. *Words in Time: A Social History of the English Vocabulary*. New York: Basil Blackwell Inc., 1988.

———. *Swearing: A Social History of Foul Language, Oaths and Profanity in English*. London: Penguin Books, 1991.

Johnson, Samuel. *A Dictionary of the English Language*. London: William Bell, 1783.

Kacirk, Jeffrey. *Forgotten English*. New York: William Morrow & Company, 1997.

Lempriere, J. *Lempriere's Classical Dictionary*. London: Milner and Company, 1887.

Love, Brenda. *Encyclopedia of Unusual Sex Practices*. New York: Barricade Books Inc., 1992.

Mackay, Charles. *Lost Beauties of the English Language*. London: Bibliophile Books, 1987.

The Merck Manual of Diagnosis and Therapy. 15th ed. Rahway, N.J.: Merck & Co., 1987.

Nare, Robert. *Nare's Glossary*. Charles Loeffler, 1825.

Partridge, Eric. *A Dictionary of Slang and Unconventional English*. New York: Macmillan Publishing Company, 1961.

———. *Origins: A Short Etymological Dictionary of Modern English*. New York: Macmillan Publishing Company, 1958.

Perry, William. *The Royal Standard English Dictionary*. Brookfield, Mass.: E. Merriam & Co., 1806.

Q.P.B. Dictionary of Difficult Words. New York: Quality Paperback Book Club, 1994.

Ray, J. *A Collection of English Words Not Generally Used*. 4th ed. London: W. Otridge, 1768.

Rheingold, Howard. *They Have a Word for It*. Los Angeles: Jeremy P. Tarcher, 1988.

Richardson, Charles. *A New Dictionary of the English Language*. London: William Pickering, 1844.

Rocke, Russell. *The Grandiloquent Dictionary*. Englewood Cliffs, N.J.: Prentice-Hall Inc., 1972.

Rodale, Jerome Irving. *The Synonym Finder*. Emmaus, Pa.: Rodale Press, 1978.

Saussy, George Stone III. *The Logodaedalian's Dictionary of Interesting and Unusual Words*. Columbia, South Carolina: University of South Carolina Press, 1989.

Schmidt, J. E. *The Lecher's Lexicon*. New York: Bell Publishing Company, 1967.

Schur, Norman W. *1000 Most Obscure Words*. New York: Facts on File, 1990.

Sharman, Julian. *A Cursory History of Swearing*. New York: Burt Franklin, 1968.

Shipley, Joseph T. *Dictionary of Early English*. Paterson, N.J.: Littlefield, Adams, and Company, 1963.

The Signet/Mosby Medical Encyclopedia. New York: Penguin Books, 1987.

Sperling, Susan Kelz. *Lost Words of Love*. New York: Clarkson Potter Publishers, 1993.

Taber's Cyclopedia Medical Dictionary. 15th ed. Philadelphia: F. A. Davis Company, 1985.

Trench, Richard C. *Dictionary of Obsolete English*. New York: Philosophical Library, 1958.

Universal Dictionary of the English Language. New York: Peter Fenelon Collier, 1898.

Walker, John. *Critical Pronouncing Dictionary and Expositor of the English Language*. New York: Collins and Hannay, 1831.

Warrack, Alexander. *The Concise Scots Dictionary*. Poole Dorset: New Orchard Editions, 1988.

Webster, Noah. *An American Dictionary of the English Language*. Springfield, Mass.: George and Charles Merriam, 1857.

Webster's New International Dictionary. 2d ed. Springfield, Mass.: G. & C. Merriam Company, 1961.

Webster's Universal Unabridged Dictionary. Merriam-Webster, 1936.

Willy, Vander, and Fisher. *The Illustrated Encyclopedia of Sex.* New York: Cadillac Publishing Company, 1950.

Worchester, Joseph. *A Dictionary of the English Language.* Boston: Samuel Walker & Co., 1873.

Wright, Joseph. *The English Dialect Dictionary.* London: Henry Frowde, 1898.

Wright, Thomas. *Dictionary of Obsolete and Provincial English.* London: Henry G. Bohn, 1857.

Zettler, Howard G. *-Ologies and -Isms.* Detroit, Mich.: Gale Research Company, 1978.